CW00854319

THE NATION THAT TRUST IN GOD

THE NATION THAT TRUST IN GOD

God Knows

Library of Congress Control Number:		2019906758
ISBN:	Hardcover	978-1-7960-3650-3
	Softcover	978-1-7960-3649-7
	eBook	978-1-7960-3651-0

Print information available on the last page.

Rev. date: 09/26/2019

To order additional copies of this book, contact:
Xlibris
1-888-795-4274
www.Xlibris.com
Orders@Xlibris.com
783271

CONTENTS

Dedication

This book, *The Nation That Trusts in God,* is completely dedicated to our one and only God, the creator of heaven and earth and all that are contained therein.

He is God, the God who was, is, and is to come. I see in my heart and hate how mankind loves and seems to worship money and power more than God. We look down on his love for us, take things for granted, and are so ungrateful to the Mighty, Supernatural Immortal, who holds the keys to our mortal lives. He is also the sole Creator; none is like unto him. He is the ultimate God who must be obeyed. I stopped writing my life story and started writing and reading his book, by his order, to the end. He is the first in my life as well as in everybody's life.

Also, this is dedicated to all those out there who will get the chance to read this book and get a change of heart to do all that God has required of them, both men and women, to live in obedience and in righteousness, to strive for heaven, and to live forever in the second world. To God be all the glory; adoration and honor belong to him. There is none like him, before him, or after him who is as glorious as he is.

He is the Creator, Savior, Protector, Deliverer, Healer, Rock of Ages, the Lily of the Valley, the Ancient of Days, Jehovah Jireh, Jehovah Shalom, the Alpha and Omega, the First and the Last, the Great I Am, and all that we can think of. He is everything, and everything is for his glory that he never shares with anyone. For he is the only one of his kind with all the powers that deserve to be reverenced and obeyed. Also, this is dedicated to all true men and women of God who are in the kingdom's business to give God all the glory he deserves.

And this is dedicated to all men and women out there who are his genuine agents: the pastors, the apostles, the reverends, the prophets, and all the people advocating for the kingdom of God, to deliver his beloved people from the bondage of Satan into heaven, the New Jerusalem, for him to be our Governor. To him alone be the glory, in the mighty name of Jesus, amen and amen.

Introduction

Many have seen the light and tried to stay out of sin, to come out with all vim to bring our brothers, sisters, sons, and daughters to the mansions being readied for us in paradise. When as many as we could be converted, Jesus will come, and the whole troubles created by Satan will come to an end. All his torments of fears and pains will end. He will be put in prison to give us peace. That will be more than anything we can imagine, full of happiness, no more sin, no more tears, death, and chaos. But this second world without the devil will be our dream come true. We will be with the Father, Son, and the Holy Spirit.

Therefore, this is worth fighting for, to redeem our own just like how Jesus came to redeem us when the same devil made all mankind short of our glory to be separated from our Father. Beloved people of God, I mean those who have seen the light, we are at war as Christians, but we are covered. So let's gather our strength and fight this battle with the help of the heavenly Father, Son, and the Holy Spirit. We are to conquer this battle and win the souls of many people possibly as we can for God's kingdom. Many souls are still confused and are struggling.

America was chosen for the whole world to migrate to, to learn at, to work in, and to feed the family back home. Though there are other countries, America has been chosen among nations like how the Israelites were chosen among all the people of God. And the founders also knew God, thanked him with celebration, and involved him in all areas of their establishment. God is different toward this nation that he has seriously endowed with many blessings so its citizens can take care of all his people and nations. Naturally, when a people or a nation is blessed by God so much, then the devil comes to play his roles to corner them since the beginning. And this devil is attacking Americans and the whole world into serious sin.

The meaning of this book is the love of people and where we go from here. God has the greatest love for people and will do anything for them. And there is an adversary, the devil, whose idea is by any means to hurt God and his children. He used to be one of his beloved angels and played it stubborn to rebel and create war between them, the Supernatural and the impostor, only to hurt those that the Father has created to replace him, the devil, in praising and worshipping him, the Father. And he is committing our great nation to be the leaders of some abominable sins while the whole world looks up to us to learn from and thrive for. What can we do now to free ourselves from these serious sins to please the Maker and be one with him?

Now humanity is in trouble for choosing to replace him and for devising so many techniques to cause various sins, using our human bodies to hurt him. It should be of the Father's interest now. The Father, knowing our frame that we are not immortal like him and are mortal and vulnerable to the devil's tricks, gave us the Bible, written by the inspiration of the Holy Spirit through various people like the disciples, prophets, apostles, and others to guide us.

Though he had been conquered by Jesus on our behalf two thousand years ago, the devil is still very stubborn, luring us into various scams just to grieve the Father and the Trinity. The devil is making humanity equally stubborn to make us regret that God had created us in the first place.

He regrets before and now. Being all-knowing, God created all things in Jesus, who came to be born like us to redeem us to himself when we were all at fault. He still lives in us to convict, convince, and convert us back for better lives because he can't afford to lose his children to this wicked guy who wants to convict us to the perpetual lake of fire waiting for him. When anybody causes any grievous sin, my heart breaks for the Father, and I think about the lake of fire awaiting us.

I might have fallen short to sin in this life race before, but for a long time now, I am trying my best to live a righteous life that's pleasing to the Father and will save me from going to hell. I am telling my children too, and I want as many people as possible, if not all mankind, to read this book. Yes, there is heaven, and there is hell also. They are both really coming.

The Father asked me to write as he is talking through me and to you like others in the Bible. Because I don't have the words and all the wisdom to write, he is with me every step of the way. And I am always crying whenever I hear about any sinful act from TV or from anybody to hurt God. Whenever I start to write this book, my heart is very broken for Father God. How could the very people he had created and loved hurt him with the sins that he had warned us of? We don't even care about him like he cares and loves us regardless.

He instructed me to write this book without any prejudice against any individual or any law, only on how we can repent and go to heaven to meet the Father for the biggest party like the one that was thrown for the prodigal son. Can human beings in general comprising that being with the one who cares so much about you with unconditional love, created you, redeemed you, and would do anything for you, to the one who wants your downfall, through various sin to disgrace your destiny and make the a world horrible for you just to take your life? My prayer is that many people, if not all, will come to know Jesus through him and to God.

This book is being written under his direction to tell us how much he cares for you and me. He wants us to think about where we are going from here. It is true. Heaven is real for the righteous, and hell is real for the sinful. So earlier, we make amends and change our mind-sets, attitudes, and lifestyles to what is best for you and me and us all. Let's be sinless.

Those who have seen the light are Christians living in righteousness for the Father. The devil really pesters our lives. But there is no turning back, and since we have built our relationships to the Father through the death of Jesus Christ, we are covered under his protection that will never allow the devil to consume us. That is why he wants us all to come to him through Jesus to join that kind of blood coverage for the kingdom.

Under his instruction, I am writing this book to connect us all back to where we belong. This is for us all, people of God, without any prejudice whatsoever; no matter our affiliations, colors, ethnic group, and beliefs, all must be protected because there are provisions made for change with time. That is why evangelists, pastors, apostles, prophets, bishops, men, and women of God are there as the agents of God, echoing to the people through the churches, televisions, crusades, and revivals. Wherever we are, we are praying that you will be found to involve yourself. The time to renew your mind for salvation is now, not tomorrow, knowing Jesus is coming soon and very soon, even if it will take us to mount a talk show to get to as many as we can reach. Reaching the lost at a cost is our kingdom's mandatory duty to assist the heavenly Father. What the Father wants us to keep in mind is where we go from here.

The fact is, he brought us here for a purpose and does not want to lose us since he had laid out rules and regulations to follow to live for him. The devil has taken over his world just to get us into going to hell with him. And this will not be profitable. He has given us first, second, and even third and other chances to be transformed since his Holy Spirit lives in us to convict us, to feel remorse, and to refrain from sin with his promptings. The Father knows he is constantly working on his children to perfection. This is just like how parents keep an eye on their children until adulthood and even continue with advice since age comes with experience.

In the pursuit of money, though necessary for some fulfillment in life and for protection against calamity, he is aware of all our needs, such as security, housing, transportation, health, feeding, clothing, and others. He then wants us, his children, to strengthen our relationship and depend on him, to get his salvation through Jesus Christ. And all the things we need will be given to us since they have been laid in place for us before we got here.

He put our needs together before he put you in your mother's womb. Yet we are to fulfill our part as his beloved. Are we not aware that he is the sole orchestrator of this whole universe and everything thereof and that he is all-knowing? He just wants us to depend on him to make all our pursuits easier so as not to fall into the temptations of the devil, which will lead us to strict judgments and possibly heaven or hell awaiting all of us.

His judgment is inescapable, and because he gave us all the chances to know the Bible through his agents, coaxing us and singing to welcome us. But we chose Satan. We cannot say we did not know or never heard anything. The main thing people have abused is the chance to make our own choices as a people he created and valued. After all the chances and we do not turn to him, then we will have ourselves to be blamed. There is going to be severe judgment in the perpetual fire, where the devil will be too. Living with puffed shoulders and with your chest out to meet the devil and his fallen angels in hell will be your worst.

No! You are too precious to end up in hell. When you see the picture discussed by the people who were near death, feel the pinch. All these great efforts are to get us out of hell. With this assessment, the Father wants us to escape this hell and come to where he is preparing for us. It is called the Paradise or the New Jerusalem. There he will rule us, and there will be no more pain, chaos, and tears, which we are sharing in

Satan's world of today, cannot be compared to that. Jesus will be on his throne, and we will be happily assisting.

It takes righteous living to be among the saints marching on to heaven to live with him forever in peace. The bottom line is, Are we living our lives running in circles to create our own confused happiness or living for the one who can give us the happiness we deserve, if only we will trust and obey? There is a broad, short way that leads to happiness, but the end is death. There is a narrow, long way that leads to struggling, but the end is abundant life to be ruled under Jesus the Messiah, leading to eternity.

Regardless of our sinful nature, if we will only renew our minds for a change to live by his rules and statutes, he is ready to forgive us and make amends. Jesus came not for the righteous, which means they were not sick, but for the sinful who were sick and needed to see the doctor. A woman who has children shows concern about them, but a woman who has no children does not care much about them. That was why the other woman who slept on her child to die had the nerve and the edge to ask King Solomon to cut another woman's baby into two. And the real mother couldn't. This is exactly what is happening between our heavenly Father who has us as his children and the devil who has no children and care only about how he can corner someone into destruction.

The fact is, by everybody reading the Bible, the earlier we make changes in our attitudes on some wild lifestyles and examine them against the ways of the enemy and become obedient to whatever the Bible is guiding us, the lesser sins we will cause. Most of us were brought up in churches, especially singers. Then when we grow up, we depart from what the church has taught us and take that of the world, leading to some TV productions that do not give any good outcome even for the children. Producing the youth who are careless about God or don't even know him follow the wild styles bred by demons from under the sea.

With this book, God is talking to the Americans, whom the world would follow as leaders that he has chosen to take care of this world through the foundations laid by our ancestors—foundations which connected him into building this nation. His involvement led to major blessings he had showered onto the modern Americans like how he had chosen the olden-day Israelites as his people and as an example to the world through how they were allowed into punishment when they sinned and how they were led out of captivity when they prayed and stayed away from sin. Then he forgives and brings us back to himself. I am doing what he is asking me, to write and also obey what he is stressing together with you, having been created together.

The same thing is going to happen to us if we do not renew our mind and stay away from our sinful nature and especially sins of abomination, like prostitution, homosexuality, lesbianism, transgenderism, and other forms of sins, which would all take us straight to hell. These mentioned ones apply to our nation, America, as the originators; and God wants to know from us Americans what went wrong as the nation that trusts in God. These mentioned ones affect him spiritually since he lives in our bodies in the form of the Holy Spirit, and we are grieving him. God and Jesus forgave, but the Holy Spirit does not forgive. Therefore, I was thinking about all my experiences and how painful it will be to God before he enjoined me to go ahead and write them all, which I was considering as all facts.

And going on to his amazement that they have forgotten what happened to some nations and the people who perished, I wrote mine first and joined his words and feelings in the new book, *The Nation That Trusts in God*.

Chapter 1

The Solid Foundation

The Father used this nation, America, like a father, to take care of all nations as a country with a big heart. That's how the Creator blessed and used this country. I love this country. For this country and many other things, I was supposed to join my fiancé here in 1973. But to the disagreement of my mom, I could not come, and she connected me to her choice.

When I completed my career school and working, I planned to come to America in 1984 to visit this country that I love so much. The states I visited were New York, Washington, Virginia, Houston, and Dallas to see things like the White House, NASA, and others. That time, I came to survey the country to come and stay there to continue my life after my divorce. But I could not leave my children; my mom couldn't hold the fort. And when my daughter completed high school, she decided to come here to go to college. Almost all of us are here now. Majority are citizens including myself leaving one now.

When a natural disaster happens, I always asked the Father why, why, many times. After some time, he started answering me. I am an evangelist, and I am prayerful. So I started having answers to my questions, and I put them together in this book. This is about how this lovely country was built on a solid foundation and what is going on now and what the Father wants us to do to maintain our position.

Though he has blessed the nation, some things don't seem right to him and need to be corrected for him to continue showering us with more blessings. He created this nation for us on his behalf. We are all his and have accounts to give as custodians for his things. We have survived with his assistance in America.

He really needs his children to live according to his commandments and statutes. He has already laid them down in the Bible to guide us. There are a lot of churches and pastors, and still a lot more people are missing the link to know him and live for him. Being a jealous God who created everything, he would not allow our adversary to continue destroying the very people who are supposed to replace him, out of sheer jealousy.

Despite natural disasters of all forms, we call Mother Nature. We don't see that they are signs and wonders of him showing us his wrath. So many things he dislikes are happening increasingly, causing him to lose us for lack of knowledge. He had to increase the usage of prophets, like he did with our ancestors, the Israelites, to reach out to the people in any means possible to claim his children no matter our sin, hence the signs of Mother Nature.

The revelation was to get a platform and echo to the American people and the world at large. As I am praying for this platform, I was told to write a book about the mission and what it is about—the importance and the benefits to mankind and why it is necessary. For his love as a Father, he will not easily give us up to the one who did not put any effort in creating us. But what the Father had created is what the devil came to steal, kill, and destroy. When he thought about so many people he had lost hell with Satan and his fallen angels, then what is the significance of the death of Jesus on the cross and the resurrection?

He is considering his Second Coming since many of his children have lost to the sin of Satan, and he is to do what he has to do to get his children back. For the Second Coming, he does not want so many to die in sin and end in perpetual fire with Satan. This is exactly what he wants to avoid, and it led him to send Jesus to bring us back to himself. With his grace, which is sufficient, and loving kindness and mercy enduring forever, Father God gives many chances for our goodness to renew our minds and make changes for the better with his help.

The foundation of this nation, from what I know, was built on Thanksgiving. "In God we trust" was declared by our forefathers, followed by "One nation, one people, under one God" on our money by one great evangelist. Then the national anthem also mentioned God throughout, like "God bless America," concluding with "God bless the people, and God bless America." All these showed how the forefathers who first discovered America reverenced God and put him first, being grateful of a land that they have discovered. They knew that they could not have done anything or could not have progressed without his divine intervention. With him comes success and victory in all the projects he is in.

This foundational call was appreciative to him to assist them every step of the way through the wars, settlement, nation building, industrial revolution, and many more. From the fourteenth century until now, America has come very far. Though many nations have developed, America was the first to develop so rapidly apart from Great Britain, where they got their independence as their masters. And now we are they are the masters in many things, as part of the blessings.

This foundational attachment allowed the Father to make this nation the head of all nations, where other nationals come to seek greener pastures to take care of families and where the majority come to seek a continuation of their education for all sorts of life and national development. Many send their knowledge back home to develop their country, like the first president of my country of origin. Others continue to stay here to help build this nation.

All these were when the pilgrims first discovered America from Britain. They did not leave God out of the big picture. They had dinner with the Red Indians, and the indigenous people had dinner with them as a way of thanksgiving to God. This is the only country in the whole planet Earth that did that to show their appreciation to God for their discovery. I heard other people had been here and left, like Portuguese and others. This celebration we have every year is for God, and that alone means a lot to him. Including all those things mentioned made the Father decide to bless and bless America.

Therefore, this nation is like Paul, who came late among the apostles of Jesus Christ but became the apostle who worked hard and wrote many books to all the churches he set up to encourage them all the time, making sure they followed the gospel. America was discovered when many nations were already in existence and bypassed them to become the first nation and the greatest nation that cares for other nations almost like how God cares for them.

Having had that recognition with God, it was their covenant with him to let them win many wars. This is the country that always tries to help the feeble countries like Vietnam, South Korea, and many others to the extent of losing their men and women. His blessing was locating them wherever they go and whatever they do. They begin with wars, industrial revolutions, mines, manufacturing, science, doctors, and health care. And now it's a computerized nation for the jet age.

Through President Kennedy, they went to the moon to give the world cell phones. You can see most of this from watching the old movies and the new movies to see how far America has come. The developments have been so rapid, and every time, new things are added, confirming the American Dream, which all nationals from other nations are coming to tap into them. This is different from other nations because the Father has specifically blessed the country based on their foundational acknowledgment. They have been blessed to be a blessing onto many, which they really do, and everybody can be somebody.

It's a solid foundation because if you recognize the owner of this work, marvel at all his handiwork, and make him first in anything on your inventions, discoveries, and projects, he directs your path and finishes the project with you very successfully. That was exactly what our forefathers, who discovered this great nation, did. Before they got here, I know some discoverers like the Portuguese and French and Holland have been here and moved on without any success. They might have heard and prepared, vowing to succeed. He is the author and finisher of everything called to be a part of their arrival, thanked him and he got too interested in the honor done for him to also make them famous, making Thanksgiving a celebration.

These acknowledgments were the Thanksgiving dinner, "In God we trust," and "God bless the people, God bless America." What he cherishes most is for people to depend on him and make him part of the mission. If you consult him before you start anything on earth, this will make him very, very happy. All the attributes, the rest were "One nation, one people, under one God." This even led God to call people from all over the whole world to come and help build this great nation since all the people as well as the land were created by him.

Every admiration was accorded to the Father God to do many things for us here in America, upgrading us to become the most powerful than other predecessors, because other nations were there before America got here. These were all the invitations for God to be involved. He blesses the nation and blesses the people who come in to help and build for greener pastures, hence the great American Dream. Aiming high, you can become whatever you want to become. Among all the nations, this is one of a kind for becoming great or achieving your dream. It does not happen so easily in many other nations, even acting. God wants his children to prosper, and that is exactly what he is doing.

Though all nations are for him, this one he was invited specifically in all angles. Even the national anthem was made to call him to confirm his blessings. He loved this, because one thing he loves his children to do is to praise and worship him and makes him special. That was what he can't do for himself, that even trees and mountains do praise him.

Exactly what our forefathers did is to give recognition to the Father Almighty as the beginning and the end of their journey arrived on this land where others have come and gone, but they decided to stay. This means that their hearts were spoken to by a higher entity for a special mission to discover the land, and that higher entity started to direct their parts to succeed.

The greatest thing they did before settling here, which contributed to the foundation to be solid, was their motivation to have thanksgiving meals with the indigenous Red Indians, who were already on the land, to give them a warm welcome. So they first gave thanks to God and ate thanksgiving meals to commemorate the occasion. This had impressed him to make the foundation solid for this nation to get footed and hold people for life encounters that bring success easier and quicker than many nations, with families helping families to survive throughout the world, especially those from poor countries.

There is no country on earth that celebrates Thanksgiving, which can only be accorded to God to let him know he is appreciated. This made him do things in our lives, continue to do more, and doing more. This is the only nation that celebrates Thanksgiving with families every November 27 of every year more than any other occasion, even more than Christmas. The families across the nation travel far and near to join their families to celebrate the Thanksgiving dinner. They put a premium on families more than anything, and God loves that.

America is a family-oriented nation and cares for their citizens, apart from killing one another sometimes. This nation gave recognition to God and gave him thanks for their discovering of this land, and this energized him to take them through all their endeavors to achieve success every step of the way to bring them this far. Their blessings were intensified as they keep on doing good just as the Father will do for his children.

So the nation that trusts in the Lord—"One nation, one people, under one God," "God bless America and God bless us," and celebrating Thanksgiving—excels with different kinds of blessings called the American Dream. This attracts people from all nations and all walks of life to come and pursue this American Dream, where anybody can become somebody by learning, acting, or doing what you can do best, your destiny being to polish to perfection.

The favor of the Lord accorded them the American Dream, the name only America had as compared to other nations. Those who pursued these dreams made it as millionaires and billionaires. Very young people can even tap into this, especially those in the movie industry. They make more movies than any other country, contributing to the economy. The various kinds of music they create compare to no nation. Sitcoms and main comedy shows and talk shows are all popular here than in any other nation. And the world loves to learn and copy or do the same things to get rich quick.

Chapter 2

The True Commitment

Those declarations in line with biblical principles, honoring and putting God first in their nation building, committed him to be with them in all their endeavors. They were committed to have mercy on other nations to the extent of fighting and losing people for their battles on having democracy for their governments. America is the first nation that started with the Israelites to put ship during the Holocaust time to bring them to settle here. People chosen by God to come to this land even added honey to the love of the nation from God. They acted on behalf of the Father God to take care of the vulnerable people on earth who were suffering and dying from other nation's wicked leadership, socialism, and communism.

They are for the whole world, looking out for their interests, just like what the Father would do. It was like he himself acting through them to take care of his children on earth. Jesus came to set us free from sin while Americans were fighting our battles from oppression. One very thing they even hated was dictatorship. From the country I know, the first leader was a dictator and a power pack and even had his university education from the United States. They were helped to topple his government in the coup d'état to free the people from tyranny and dictatorship around 1966. I was then in elementary school to know of this.

This nation got its name as the first country among all the nations of the world from its major commitment for mostly humanitarian assistance in terms of saving human life—the fighting of wars and losing its own people, giving monetary assistance, evacuation of other nationals to American grounds, including the typical example of bringing the Jewish from the Holocaust to settle them here. They brought the refugees from Somalia to help them settle in Rochester, Minnesota, and did other unnoticed humanitarian assistance that no country can come close to these things, which won them the first world position all by the favor of God.

The world saw their commitment, boldness, and actions, trying to let the world follow democracy instead of communism and socialism. Democracy is the best government of the people, by the people, and for the people and allows the people to make their choices instead of through intimidation and dictation. The bottom line is all about the people's welfare and well-being. This means they care about the people, while others are power packs that pocket riches. Instead of the people, they and their interest matter. Of course, some favor and fight for the poor and the middle class, and others favor the rich.

I would have not believed this until I came to see and hear things in politics myself. Due to our serious commitment to the world, the whole world viewed us as their leader to rescue them in any situation, which of course we do. Still, the working class and the middle class are not favored in terms of living standards, especially when it comes to health care and taxes, as compared to the rest of the world. People's sickness and diseases cost more money, and we are to have insurance to make our care easier. My point here is, God in his creation knows some will be rich, and they are to take care of the poor. This is happening in other countries. Here, too, some are doing but should be more than anticipated and involve themselves, like stronger holding the weak for food, shelter, and clothing, including fitting in the society and visiting the prisoners and praying for them to get a change of heart.

With the way we care so much for others, we should set our country in favor of the poor before we consider helping others in any situation. This is so that we don't become hypocrites and become our brother's keeper like what the Father wants us to do. He said, "As I have loved you, you should love them the same way I have loved you." This is the meaning of being your brother's keeper. That is what God wants us to do, and blessed be those who keep this love forever. This nation is well-known for its commitment for benevolence, giving assistance whether it is in war, giving health assistance, and challenging a dictator to free his people. We are the leaders of democracy against socialism and communism and dictatorship.

With any of the natural disasters happening in another country—like hurricanes, tsunamis, earthquakes, storms, and others—America will be their first responders with their aids before other countries even come to join. They are fighting for democracy for all nations to free us from socialism and communism. It is their passion to get democracy for all developing countries. Americans go by rule of law and freedom of expression for their citizens. The dream here is, anybody can become somebody according to their expertise.

The American Dream, which people from all nations and spheres of life come and pursue, is part of the commitment in leadership. They are also committed to education, how people can improve education through loans from the government to live a better life for nation building and productivity. Education gives more knowledge to thrive and improve the national economy. The more the people have knowledge to produce, the more the people have better life like health care, industries, and others for the national productivity to strengthen the economy for nation building with solid infrastructure, like bridges, roads, and schools.

The health care is good to heal with best doctors, but the health care in this nation is the most expensive in the world. There are Medicare and Medicaid, yet many people have health insurance to assist them for the health-care cost. The current government should do something about it by passing the health-care law to favor many. I am bringing this up because of the way we care for others in other nations. We have to solve ours in all levels of life to fully complete our status as the first nation. Other than that, outsiders will look at us as hypocrites. But the current administration, being headed by President Obama, gives some affordable health care, being the first in history to help the people and the poor.

In any developed country like ours, the rich pay for fair share in taxes to pay for the country's major developments of infrastructure, the security system, and many more. This country used to be the first in all these developments, and now other nations are coming to overtake us. That is why it is necessary for fair taxes for all and not only on middle income, which I am a part of. And I know what I am talking about, for whenever I get my income, I check the taxes. Let's pray for the rich to pay their fair share for the country they love that made their fortune. Many are even ready and waiting for the administration to bring them and are willing to pay.

Majority of the rich also understand and embrace this and are doing great like the Microsoft man. He is being blessed, and his riches are increase while he also keeps on giving to the poor. This is the exact thing that pleases our Father in heaven, whose obligations are to make sure the people he created are all living with all the necessities to make their lives better and to stop crying to him. He is responsible for our needs and solves our problems, if only we will cling to him. Nevertheless, he is the only one who cares about us. No one else cares.

The law of giving is better than receiving. The more you give, the more our Father who created all things will bless you that you can't get a place to contain them. But continue to give to make others comfortable. So when you finish your term and you go up there, you can give a good account. It would not be like the rich man and Lazarus, who was in Father Abraham's bosom. There, the rich didn't count a thing, and he found it hard to quench his thirst and get a message to his family in the world, that it was too late. Beloved, don't let it be too late for us, and plan well for your own comfort.

When we leave our wealth to the next of kin, with all our invested riches, we might not know how properly he or she will be managing our monies. The bottom line will be using our own money with the ideas you think is right for your sweat, struggles, and hard work, which led you to your wealth, while you are alive, to your satisfaction before your term expires.

With the way the whole country is committed to other countries, so should individuals be committed to one another among ourselves. And so many people do that in our daily activities, like heroes saving others from situations that could kill in different ways. They bring them to TV shows like Steve Harvey to thank them with tears. So many people are heroes, and to the national heroes like the army, navy, and the air force, we are grateful to them all. Therefore, we would employ our big corporations, companies, and wealthy people to do for the people as the Father would require of them to bless others.

They forget their political background just for the interest of the great America, which God himself has blessed so much among modern nations. The country within countries other countries took our steps and are also coming up, but there is only one America, which is standing. Regardless, the rich should continue to help to keep us standing and striving.

Many individuals have formed companies to take care of disabled people and are concerned on various forms of disability. And these are usually the responsibility of the government. The American government is one committed government that cares for the people with disability who are helping their families, including children in foster care and foster homes.

Children are taken care of before they are even adopted, including the abandoned children, all the things God cares about. They are the major reason for our blessings. The Father cherishes those who take care of others to settle them from crying, which breaks his heart, just like a parent who could not feed his or her children. Those doing drug abuse, shelters, for homeless, and many assisted programs from the government whenever someone is bold to set up a company, especially in any special need which is meaningfully being assisted by the government financially.

The world really respected America and made them flood here in their numbers than any country. I can't figure out where in the world this is done more properly than in America. I know Great Britain and Germany are also doing well. People feel at home here, apart from the killings. And yet come what may, they still feel proud and feel at home here more than elsewhere.

The people are the government and the helping hands that empower the government to do things for them to enable the people to help families back home to survive and to leave God at peace out of crying and by praying. On average, one out of each family leaves for abroad to support their families back home. And it was God who planned it like that. Every individual has a potential hidden in him or her to do as a talent. That is why if, for some reason, one could not become normal to deliver, then we are to help him or her to survive till their term has ended. If they deliver, then they become our heroes or our stars. So the Father said, "As I have loved you, go and love your neighbors like yourselves. Love the greatest of all to live."

Father God loves all his people; hence, he gives rain and air to both righteous and sinful, knowing that one day, the sinful would be converted. Muhammad Ali said, and I quote, "Be selfless and not selfish." He was not only a boxer but also an inspirational speaker who was very helpful to all kinds of people. Therefore, coming to this world out of nothing, what you do makes a difference in someone's life. Help the government and our nation. Don't die with your potential. Leave a legacy, die in peace, and give good accounts to your Father God on how committed are you to your work here on earth for his appraisal. Everybody has potential, and everyone can do something to help make a difference in the world as a better place.

There are so many areas for everyone to play specific roles for. Churches, companies, hospitals, businesses, and the seat of the government do their responsibilities, all helping to make a difference. For example, doctors, nurses, and health-care workers make the formation of hospitals complete. The president, senators, governors, FBI, and all other officials contribute to help manage the country. The churches, with their evangelists, pastors, apostles, prophets, and bishops, are also managing the Churches for salvation and the eternity of the people. We should all do whatever we know best to contribute and do our part for a blessed nation building.

If you are not within the categories I have mentioned, you still know within yourself what completes your personality to do and make someone happy, laugh, and liberated. Parents have a responsibility to bring up their children to be on their feet from birth through nursery, kindergarten, primary school, high school, and college. Even until they get married, parents remain at the background. Children have a responsibility to care for their parents throughout their old age and sickness till they pass away.

Companies and businesses put jobs together for us to get work and be able to make ends meet, including small businesses and their roles. Then all are put together for grading before the biggest boss, our God, to see who goes to heaven with the roles we played.

Chapter 3

Found Favor and Blessings

The foundational commitment I have mentioned include Thanksgiving, "In God we trust," "God bless America, God bless the people," even "One people, one nation, under one God," and not forgetting the national anthem, which showed very great for God's recognition that no country has done before and will ever do. This earned the country a very big favor from the Father God, leading to blessings that contributed to what we have today to be valued.

One thing the Father cannot do for himself after creating heaven and earth and everything that it contains is praising, worshipping, admiring, honoring, and putting him in the first place of everything that we do as his people. He wants us to acknowledge him and do that for him, including the mountains, birds, trees, and all his creation, praising him to feel appreciative, happy, and great. For his love, he is very appreciative too. And that was the effort our ancestors did for the foundation to make this nation great among nations regardless.

A country like this should be very careful in doing things, for the whole world looks up to us. And the Father also is waiting for our actions to bless them, especially the good ones. The people he had created are supposed to love him, live like him, and go according to his commandments and statutes. Yet the other entity would not and has been an obstructionist since the day he was thrown down into the earth from heaven. He always has his fallen angels, like his agents, acting for him, just as the churches are also acting and advocating for our Father God Almighty, who was and is to come. The problem is that the Creator creates, heals, delivers, protects, supplies, and comforts, while the other steals the skills and destroys them. Now in your clear mind, who should be obeyed? Whether we obey or not, that day would soon catch up with us. That is the reason why every minute counts.

After faithful ancestors laid the foundation from Great Britain, whom I heard were connected to King James of Britain, who also helped with the Bible translation, let us understand that the people knew their God. The people who know their God will do exploits. Then came also from Germany another people with the belief to join the British founders. Then all people from many nations migrated to join this new nation.

Later, the blacks also came here as slaves from Africa. And they all fought in the war with the indigenous Red Indians, who were occupying the land that is now the United States of America and comprised of fifty big states, outstanding in the world like Paul, who came late but did tremendous work. Instead of the blacks equally enjoying, they are constantly being killed for petty reasons, and they are also killing themselves for reasons best known to themselves. One thing our adversary does best is making us unhappy.

A young African man with his mother and two sisters completed engineering and got shot in an argument in the black neighborhood. The country we love to come to for greener pastures still is so scary that we live here with only prayers to survive.

With this alone, we can't leave Jesus outside our lives but inside us to protect us from situations before they even arrive. Even this alone should get us so close to our Father God. Serving him with all our hearts, let's live in righteousness to turn hatred from our hearts. Hatred is of the devil, and love is of God. Jesus never left hatred.

Then there was another war to get independence from their masters, the British, and they won to get independence. Since they put God first ahead of them, they won the wars among themselves from state to state with President Abraham Lincoln and others on the segregation of the blacks as slaves. All these were won because they did things with God, which was favorable to the Father. In all their deliberations, God was in their midst at all times.

Then they brought the Israelites in ships here in America from Germany for settlement. This also entails many blessings from their foundational acknowledgment. All that they did led them to be favored by the Father, and the blessings kept on flowing. These attracted people from all nations, coming here to follow the American Dream, that is, to share these blessings. They come to follow these American Dreams, and if you are lucky to tap into it, you easily become millionaires and billionaires. They are directions from God himself.

There are a lot of stardom works in the country. They are the movie industries in this nation, which is more than any other nation in the world. They are very profitable. Also, education here is like farming in Africa around the era of baby boomers. The parents were mainly farmers. And here, if you don't have anything at all, not even basic education up to at least high school, other countries may call secondary school and career schools, as well as small businesses and big companies, to do your own skill work.

Wall Street, for the investors even from different countries, is trying to make money. The contributing factor is that nobody should be lazy or do nothing or you get kicked out from an apartment, unless you have some sort of inheritance from your parents or grandparents. Everybody is trying to get his or her share of the blessings the Father has endowed us with. Everybody is doing something to survive; the aged and the sick are being cared for, and the rich are opening companies for the middle- and lower-income people to work, like all hands on deck.

I knew and visited other countries, and a lot of people are seeking greener pastures in other developed countries like Great Britain, France, Germany, and others; but this country is one of a kind. The entertainment industry pays and cannot be compared with any other country, and they all come here to make a fortune. Music and basketball were first dominated by the blacks, but now by all, and this is all because of our acknowledgment of the Father, leading us to the great blessings as oneness in the Lord, who is no respecter of persons.

I don't think that if we have started being all that sinful, he would have led us to all the various blessings we are facing right now. Even in the middle of a crisis, the nation is blessed. Now our forefathers are gone. A lot more people from all backgrounds are flooding into the country, the rich country with all kinds of jobs to offer—like Tom, Dick, and Harry jobs. Everybody prayed for visas and were given before we got here and survived.

Things have never been easier, unless you pray hard and God will divinely give you one. Their work and legacy won us world recognition. The worldview on us is like America will come and save us despite how badly we want democracy to reign instead of socialism, communism, and dictatorship, along with gun supply, which may paint us badly sometimes. Still we are recognized as the leaders the world is looking up to, apart from the colonial masters, Great Britain. Now where are we heading toward? What are too much blessings turning us into? As a nation that trusts in the Lord, now what are we doing? Many allow the root of money, being the root of evil, to commit all unspeakable sins like we have no God.

Chapter 4

The World Recognition

The world recognition pertaining to us Americans is that we are the world leaders in everything you can think of. We are masters of world fashion, technology, industry, manufacturing, education, health, music, ministries, and many more. Though others might have learned from us and are challenging us, our foundation is our pillar that the Father considered to bless us. No matter what any country does, without our kind of foundation, they can't beat us. For we will be all known as a country that might be good in doing things but not around things like the United States of America winning the name *the American Dream.*

Therefore, we should not be complacent and think it's our hard work or integrity. It is our great ancestral foundation, which brought God first into their vision to set good goals and to complete their big mission for us to follow and complete with power to become great. This means we have been blessed inside and outside. All nations were created by the Almighty, but some are highly blessed than others. Thank God for our forefathers.

Then we became like a big tree that every bird comes to perch its nest. In other words, we are a country where all people go to take refuge, yet we should beware that we don't step over some boundaries of the Originator, the Owner himself. Remember, we are all citizens of the kingdom above, as well as citizens of where we were born, lived, or migrated.

Wherever we might be, we are to respect the authority and obey the rules, including job places and schools. If we obey as the children of the kingdom like God accorded unto us, whoever will overlook with hatred or racism and maltreatment will be an enemy to God himself to fight the battles till we win. So always we should play our role with excellence and godliness, like children of the kingdom anxious to go to heaven, as we are in transit.

The Originator is of a higher entity. Too much wealth, too much entertainment, too much happiness, and too much partying make us forget our foundational rules—who created us, where we come from, and where we are going from here. We have all begun to ponder over these as one people, one nation, under one God before our blessing turns out to be something different. Now it is not our technology, our movies, our Wall Street stocks, our education, our health care, or anything that makes us proud but our relationship with our Father, to put him first.

If, included in any project and with the first honor, he makes sure to bring you to success, those who came here first, were very smart to know this secret and made a point to do so. Many countries were discovered before America, but they gained that recognition and honor.

The foundational commitment had an impact on us to do only what is good to other countries, making us the masters. They follow our examples and do what we do for they know we are good and caring people. If anything happens to others, America will act first and pull others to join for action. Two wars in Afghanistan and Iraq have caused us the lives of our young men and women. And only a few countries would want to make a commitment like that, not even all in the United Nations. God bless the leaders who would protect our heroes. When we visit many cemeteries, we see the graves of young men and women from nineteen years and up who have forfeited their full lives ahead of them. The love and care for others—not many countries would do that. Many soldiers have died already, and no more.

This probably made President Obama retrieve them back for the wars we never won, but only losing lives and money. It resulted to strikes that cost us money to save human lives. Sometimes using wisdom is better than using weapons of war to solve the same situations. Settlement between countries with wisdom saves lives and money. Wars are now becoming obsolete and no more; the answer is, many wisdoms are applied than hatred.

This strategy is good for the parents and families of our heroes. Those who probably don't have people in the army may not care who dies. The fact is, one people, one nation, under one God should have feelings for one another, like in 9/11 and like the shooting in the church at South Carolina around 2015 or 2016, along with the terrorist shooting in Orlando on June 10, 2016, and many more. We always mourn with one another. We love oneness between us in times of crises and disasters. One thing in the Lord is that disasters and crises could be stopped by Him who made them happen with righteousness. Recently, seventeen children and adults died in Parkland, Florida, around February 13, 2018. How many times would parents be hurting for killings?

Death by terrorism has been going on in London, Paris, and Belgium, yet we are the number 1 target by these terrorists. Why? Has our recognition won us enemies? No! It is our pulling away from the One whom we were proud to do our business with and made him lead us. When we became successful, we pull away, thinking it is our own strength, power, and ideas. Relying on this with too much freedom is now allowing many sins here.

Sin (self-interest now) includes various sins that drive our Father away from the original project that was laid down between him and our forefathers, who first came here and got him involved.

Now, though we are recognized, we are suffering in many areas, like the Father is angry with you and me, but we are not taking notice. We keep on bouncing back and always are on our feet without checking the root cause. We should continue to build on this foundation with the fear of God and his righteousness. Being reliant on God is the remedy.

Whenever the Father is angry with his children, he causes things to happen to call our attention for us to renew our minds and come back to make it up to him, because he is a forgiving Father. You will know this if you read about his people, the Israelites, in the Bible. We find peace and add it to our recognition, and nobody can give peace apart from our heavenly Father. He gives peace that passes all others; peace made by men doesn't last.

The hope in the Lord brings joy and peace. Peace does not come with consistent sin. Our loving Father is always in the business of forgiveness and unconditional love. God does not give peace with sin reigning in a country. Despite other countries that might be going through some stuff, the leaders might be power-packed to do odd things while America is always defending them, making the difference and making their citizens feel liberated. What about here? Let's take care of ourselves first with the reverent love of God and his righteousness.

The world had benefited a lot of goodness and kindness from us to the extent of going to war to lose lives for other countries and offer food assistance and refugee settlements, which had all contributed to world recognition, including businesses and investments as well as care for our citizens and seniors. Apart from the cost of health care, gun violence, terrorist attacks, the enmity between us and others and among ourselves, the police and the young black males, the lives here are more interesting. And with how we welcome other countries with the rule of law, we should let them work to keep others safe. He is not happy on how some have been constantly being killed and going free. Their hands are tainted with blood for proper judgment coming from the mightiest judge, who entails the severest punishment.

This recognition will be forever, for what we have for other countries, no country comes close. United States moves before Britain, France,

Canada, and Scandinavia. That is why there are strings attached to our recognition. Whatever we do, the world follows our steps as world leaders. Remember, if it is good, they pick; if it is bad, they pick. The good examples are the ones that are beneficial to our Father God. Having begun with him, we are to continue with him. How many countries are killing their citizens like America?

Since our ancestors build the foundation with his concern, we are to make sure to do things and not set him aside. Otherwise, this will put him to wrath, and he had shown them to us through various things to be discussed soon. Can we consider and make possible changes? Many changes will stop some evil happenings to give us peace, which is the truth. We can't serve two masters, being money and God. Serving God first brings the light into our soul's spirit to manifest in our physical body. Serving money and greed is for the fresh to doom.

Instead of always losing and rebuilding and losing many lives, deaths could be avoided. All that we are did not come by our own efforts. He honors those who put their trust in him and recognize him. He has the power to make things happen to benefit us, for God is an all-knowing Father, all-planning, all-giving, all-choosing of leaders. And every good and perfect gift is from him.

The time to take a deep breath and include him in our daily activities, businesses, and our governance is better. The earlier we start seeing the world like our ancestors saw America from the foundation, the better, and to include him or accept that some higher entity brought us here and can take us from here too. Let's start praying too. Therefore, we can't cut him off from any of our deliberations in either individual life situations or for the whole nation, making him first see the troubles ahead of us and get ready with solutions before they arrive.

He is always with us as our companion, closer than even a friend, our companion who cares so much about our encounters and wants to be part of the solution if only we will allow him. He is very happy that we lean and rely on him to do our things for us. I have gone through tons of troubles, but he is always there to put me through. Because I know him, you know him, America knows him before, we should know him again. Others have hooked on to him no matter what, but according to the declaration, we are to keep him in everything we do, not forgetting that "in God we trust."

The earlier we stop doing things wrongly and making it up to him again, the quicker he forgives, protects, and promotes us back to our great recognition. It will be better to renew our minds and not lose guard and track of the ancestral foundational benefits that brought us the American Dream we loved and recognized, and we should include him as the head of all things done. He would want us to be totally dependent on his promises to strengthen for today for him to bring us hope for tomorrow. He even cares about birds and flowers.

He gave human knowledge for computers. He had computerized all our data with him over there since the day you were clothed in blood in your mother's womb, and he laid everything he wants you to become and do and nicely watched. Your obedience with all he wants you to do just allows him to just click the necessary buttons for what you want to happen without sweat. Finding answers to our problems only leads us to frustration and depression, stopping us to pray and read our Bibles to do the right thing to connect his link for the clue.

According to those pastors, God has been revealing to them that the rapture is around the corner. A revelation by one living witness said Jesus was crying and showing him many churches that are deceiving the congregations like the churches are for God and that many churches are operating under occult. Some congregations are just churchgoers and not Christians. Together, the pastors plus members, only 1 percent is going to heaven, and the 99 percent are going to hell. And Jesus was crying, crying for the painful death and crying for losing us. This is very scary. What are we going to do now? Just make sure to go to heaven.

He continues the revelation, saying that Jesus said America is on fire and Britain is on smoke, and I am adding that the whole world is watching with devastation on where to turn to, since apart from God, the world also looks up to mainly these countries for our eye opening to be comfortable with our lives as the world masters, giving birth to immigration. Many would travel to learn or to work for greener pastures and feed families back home. Many migrated here with this mind-set, which has worked for many who go back after retirement.

Those who have witnessed these signs have seen miniature hellfire and heaven, and hearts are broken, not knowing where we belong. We think we are doing the right thing, but they may not be enough to make us candidates to heaven. That is why Jesus, who cares so much for us, is continuously sounding and cautioning through others to warn us that what is ahead of us is the reality and that there's no more time to waste. Just start living our lives with humility, forgiveness, and righteousness, like Jesus with his repentance, praying for his guidance.

Chapter 5

Filled Churches

Despite filled churches, there are still a lot more people who have not heard or ever known God; rather, they consult mediums, sorcerers, and palm readers, more agents of Satan and his fallen angels. Instead of going to church for life directions, hundreds of churches are all filled up when you constantly watch Trinity Broadcasting Network (TBN). And to compare the difference, I also watch entertainment Televisions for my observation. Some lead us into sin.

Weighing the current situation of the jet age, Generation Y, and Generation Z, it is not surprising that the world is going haywire due to technologies, computers, and more and more entertainments, which are also making money fast, especially in this country. Being a baby boomer like me, you know exactly what I am talking about. Money is not bad, but the way and method use might be evil, which can even make us greedy, leading us into sin.

After you get them, then they become a curse that follows you till you will not be happy anymore, and it can cause you to commit suicide, which also goes on too much in our beloved country, America. These filled churches comprise of baby-boomers, and other generations like X, Y, and Z, many of the young generations I mentioned are chasing lives and are refusing to take time to learn properly from their parents.

And for the lack of knowledge my people perish God told the Israelites and to modern Americans. It is the duty of those who filled the churches to pray and to draw in those in the other industries who might not know God properly to come to church to know their Father God, Jesus the Redeemer, and the Holy Spirit, the companion to get us closer to the kingdom. It is better to add Jesus to the entertainment industry and, of course, to any other industry to eliminate sinful stuff to please him. In anything we do, we should make sure to please him.

Money is a blessing from the Father, but the way you chase money and forget your Father is evil. For if you get money so young without knowing him, then you turn to the world for happiness out of chasing money. They leave home early without any maturity from parents to chase the world packed with problems for happiness. Without mature minds and experiences come a price—self-made happiness to the side of the devil who loves it.

When the happiness they are looking for fails them, then they resort to short lives and death, for money doesn't give the required happiness. Only the orchestrator of this world knows the kind of happiness needed for his children, like the one he predestined us for. He wants us to seek him first and his kingdom. After that, he will give us what will give us inner peace, for the spirit that will manifest requires physical happiness.

It's different from the one we want, yet we always think we are too smart compared to this mighty God, who knows them all and can give all to mess up our lives. The devil is a typical liar and destroyer of our lives. The adversary is always accusing us about what we did wrong before God to get a chance to do to us what he did to his job. His other name is "brother, the accuser," seriously attacking pastors and agents of God with all manners of temptations to get your soul to his side in hell.

All the facts of being smarter than our master is because of *self-interest now* or sin, which is from Satan and his agents, who are spirits that use human bodies to do various known abominable sins to make our Father miserable. Since he cannot afford to lose his children, he will always hold his temper for you and me to reconnect us to the church and be introduced back to him for eternal salvation, liberation, and reconnection to the Father.

Reconnection to the Father for salvation will be the Father's interest now to have peace on earth and contributions to win more souls for his kingdom, with us being his partners here on earth while he is in heaven watching over us. This helps us to stay away from the flesh and live in the Spirit, then spend our ages gracefully with advanced in years and make it to heaven to meet with Jesus—the Savior, Messiah, Anointed Mediator, Advocate, and Intercessor. Who is making sure his death on the cross to pay the heaviest price would not go to waste if we continue to live here to satisfy the flesh? He is constantly pleading on our behalf.

Many times, when things happen, we call them Mother Nature, and who gives the chances for that Mother Nature to occur? It's our own Father, who has been yelling to us with signs of anger that it is time to stop and think. Enough is enough. Though he forgives, sin is the one thing he wants to have zero tolerance, reminding us to get closer to talk or to pray to him and behave like people who were created by him and in his likeness, not for the devil.

Truly, anytime there is a tragedy, we become vulnerable and run to the church. Do we always have to sin and wait for tragedy, or do we stay in righteousness and talk to our Father not to bring disasters? These filled churches, with their pastors, apostles, bishops, evangelists, and all Christians in the United States and the world at large, have got work to do—serious work to do. That is to bring the lost sheep back to the shepherd where they belong, to secure them from those spirits who are using their bodies to sin to get them into hell, and to shame the devil, who can also give you money to get your soul. The obstructionist, Satan, who never wants any happiness for the Father and his children, is the reason why when you are standing in the light, stand firm and pull someone to your side. Convince more people and pray for them to join you in the light, for one can't see in the darkness. Though not all are sinful, but many.

We need the passion to assist one another, for the good Father will give us big rewards for that. He wants us to be there for one another, but not the survival of the fittest, being automatic partners to be our brother's keeper and ease the problems of Satan's contamination of his children against him. That is part of the reasons for our dwelling here on earth, for the stronger to support the weaker in all life encounters, like security, shelter, clothing, food, and all the necessities of survival. Then our heavenly Father, too, will be there for us and support us all, then bless you to be a blessing unto others.

There is no way he wants any of his children go to hell with that opponent. He rather wants us all to meet him in convoy in heaven. All hands should be on deck without any further delay. The signs of Mother Nature are signaling us how the end is getting closer and closer while nobody has the specific time in view; we need to prepare. All of Mother Nature's disasters—like twisters, tornadoes, storms, hurricanes, lightings, earth slides, and others—are signs of the end of time.

His wrath is unfolding. Can't we sense them? Rather than losing people and houses and things before we run to church, we should ask ourselves why they are so frequent here as compared to other nations. Once in a while, one will happen somewhere, but it is very rampant here. Why? All beloved children of God who have seen the light and have known the Bible are aware of what is guiding us, and we should be able to bring those in darkness to join us in the light equally to see God the Father, the Son, and the Holy Spirit, being the Trinity.

The fact is, Father God created us all for himself and for the light. The opponent, Satan, did not do any creation, but because he is envious of us—from the love God took from him for us—then we became his target. He and his fallen angels got to use our bodies as they are spirits that cause all kinds of sins to make the Father angry and to get us into the fire with them.

Remember, he is aggressive, and he started with Adam and Eve to make them fall right from the Garden of Eden. Through that, we were redeemed by Jesus, and Satan is still trying to torment us with sin to bring us down by any means possible again. Jesus has not yet come because our sins, instead of diminishing, kept on growing to grieve God and make Satan happy since he doesn't care about us.

Let's all wake up to the fight and get our people to the light of God, where we are all predestined to be before we were created. We belong to the light and not the darkness. It wouldn't be easy bringing someone from his or her habitual position. We were created just to listen and take it slow, talking candidly to the one you could talk to, to convert to the light. Don't make him or her feel bad. Be mindful in your mind-set, with your intentions to gradually reach your goal in converting them.

Before you start any assignment of bringing somebody or a family member or a group of people, pray and commit them to the Holy Spirit to be with you to convict, convince, and convert all your converts, all those you talked to, and lead them to Jesus. The greatest Spirit of God has the power to change any situation of any child of God to the Father's side. We are all the Father's property, purchased by the most precious blood of Jesus Christ, the Messiah and the Anointed One, his only begotten Son.

In any case, do not pass judgment knowing we were once there and were saved by grace through Jesus. This grace of God is looking to locate his children for salvation, which has been made ready for our repentance to become new creations by accepting Jesus as our Lord and Savior and by believing for correction. The grace will make things that are good for us by our faith in the Father, and our faith will lead us to be at peace with him. The hope will bring us faith to give us joy and peace if we depend totally and trust in the Lord.

Those in darkness try to create their own happiness then end up in reckless and sinful life, which takes them early to their graves, mostly through suicides. Who would not want to his live to the fullest? Only the Father can give us peace that surpasses all understanding and can give us longer lives, but only when we get closer and depend on Him. Something someone can't help may lead him to sin. And the time for serious evangelism by all Christians is now. The more souls we win, the sooner Jesus is coming to get us from this devil's world to the New Jerusalem. I have started on three social media sites and sharing of tracts. What about you?

For the Father is grieving for a lot more of his children who are drifting to the enemy in the world, losing them. That is why Jesus has not come yet. Now, as partners, this is what I see that we can do to help. Whenever I see some things going against the Father, my heart breaks with tears, and I pray for him to forgive us and change us to conform to his likeness, to live like how he wants us to live, and to please him and benefit us. Because we are his image and not the image of Satan, who created nothing but destroys everything.

The Bible educated us about God and his creation and how he handed over to us to be accountable to him, how Jesus came, and how he is coming again. The problem is how the death and resurrection of Jesus is, instead of benefiting us, now being wasted. The time to concentrate on refraining from sin and dragging our future into the perpetual fire with the enemy is now. Let's stop him from winning. He lost the battle two thousand years ago. Jesus defeated him. Why does it seem like he is winning now? We should also not allow them to remain in the darkness to perish. Now we do not lack knowledge. We are aware of what we are facing, and we are to work on it for others to emulate Jesus and complete from what he left for us.

Looking at all the congregations in all the churches in the world, if there could be serious love like how Jesus told us to love as he had loved us, we are taking it upon ourselves to do a serious revival to continuously win souls. A lot more people will come to the light. Now we know, and we should lead them to know the biblical principles too—to overcome temptation over sin and to teach them to grow in love for the Creator.

A lot more souls are in limbo, a lot more souls are hanging in balance, and we are to answer as Christians.

When one sheep went missing, Jesus left the ninety-nine and went looking for the one, making sure the hundred were intact. Supposing Jesus comes now, how many souls is he going to find saved and intact? That is why he is still not here yet. Looking through television to view this world is heartbreaking to God, and there are those in the light and people trying to create their own happiness and how they end up. And if we sit on the fence as Christians too, Jesus will not come soon to set us free and to lock Satan in a pit. It's that simple. Churches should make tracts for members to share at your free time.

Get their addresses and phone numbers to follow up with them to make sure they come to Jesus, who left as he anointed the twelve disciples and gave them power to go preach the gospel to set the captives free from bondage and heal the sick and solidify churches. This is to be done in greater dimension to be able to save more souls. There are many churches of Jesus Christ now that will do the same thing for Jesus. Therefore, all Christians, let's get to work and be our brother's keeper. The king promised to return, but he can't come if we haven't been able to win more and more souls. Truly, more souls are getting lost and going to hell with Satan, who cares less about us.

Part of the hell suffering even starts here on earth. If you fail to surrender to the only one who cares for the preparation for your soul and spirit, your final days will start with suffering from sickness and diseases, with painful experiences that you might not get a cure for, for the situation is where one would even prefer death to end them all. That would be the time you will review in your mind's eye all the crimes and sins you performed when you were healthy. You would regret bitterly if you could come back to make changes, and it will be too late.

Now the money could not save you because the doctors might not have a cure. And the money too, you will leave them when you go, showing that, after all, money is not the answer. The answer is you did not agree to live by them. And death too doesn't mean you have finished.

The apostle Paul explained in Revelations 8–20 how they were revealed to him and how the end will be occurring with various angels and their rules to the sound of some trumpets. Some fearful creatures will each come to perform the task to torture and torment humans and the earth for years before God gives the final judgment to send you to your destination of torment.

This will be the plight of the carnal, wicked men whom the Bible says are not going to spend even half of their days living with open eyes. Be mindful of the physical torture awaiting us. All power belongs to God. Indulgence in any other power of the adversary will be digging your own torture. And at that time, our Father did all that he could, but some of us escaped the salvation, thinking they are on top. Being on top with evil wealth and not the blessings of the Lord, who alone can give power to get wealth, is more dangerous.

Chapter 6

What Went Wrong?

What really went wrong? After all our toils, fighting of wars (both world wars and civil wars), coal mining, industrial revolution, great Depression, independence, various technology, Nasser to the moon, World Trade Center, education, health care, Wall Street stocks for money, insurance companies, pharmaceutical, and many more inventions, the Father has been with us in every step of the way and direction for success. Seeing us through victory upon victory, helping us to make headway, and appreciating our ancestral acknowledgment showed how He cares about us. Then what went wrong now?

Complacency, knowing it all, depending on our capability that we can do them all on our own, integrity, and power make it seem that we don't need the Father anymore at this jet age. Probably our Ancestors needed Him for their own foundation and not for us. This realization made us so ungrateful to the Father, who has always been with his children. And when they became equipped, they don't know him anymore, just like how the Israelites were playing with him back and forth with his heart for his children, just like parents and their children in those days and now. This is such an ungrateful attitude to show to the one who is being good to you.

The Father's love never fails. He is compassionate, forgiving, merciful, and has a loving kindness that endures forever. He is patient

for all our commitments, gives ample time and room to renew our minds, and makes amends. Happiness, entertainment, and money give birth to some behavioral changes, not considering the needs of the Father who put us here and helped us and is still helping us. Human nature, many times now, shows that we are ungrateful.

These Churches are there. TBN is showing and preaching worship and Praises throughout the country and the world at large with twenty-four seven programmers, plus many other stations are in progress. Still many things are going on, like people being careless, ignorant, or naive. And that was what went wrong, which offended the Father God. More souls are in limbo and hang in the balance. For those who have never even heard of the Bible, Jesus, and salvation, let the partners of God reach these lost souls as fast as we can.

Sometimes he tells us to refrain from sin, which though he forgives but had wished zero sin. He causes some things to remind us that he is coming, and things are reaching a peak that we need to stop and make changes for him. But we only see that time is money, and money is not the answer to our happiness but only the answer to our necessities. Total happiness can come from only God with inner peace. He knows the kind of blessings we deserve to live, being reliant on him on every area of our lives as a hedge of protection, deliverance, and supplier of all our needs. He always wants all the glory to himself, being a jealous God.

The answer to our lives' happiness depends on God, who knows we need it by surrendering to him first. And we think we are so smart to find our own happiness, going in circles. This is, of course, going on with us today. The old folks did not see money in that way but saw it as one of life's necessities, which could not change them. When money comes, they lived life longer instead as they kept on regarding the Father God as the ultimate. The fastest lifestyle leaving God out to our own things under our own power has to do with many things going wrong. Yet who knows better than him? He is given the chance to come back whenever.

We feel like coming is not too late than to lose our Father in eternity to the enemy's camp. He really wants that to happen to all humanity, to tell the Father that "the people you created to replace me are still as bad as I am, the devil." And this is what the Father hates to happen. His influence let Adam and Eve fell, and Jesus redeemed the descendants of Abraham. We are probably going to fail if we don't renew our minds and make it back to Jesus and the reconciliation the Son won for us. We could lose our rights as the descendants of Abraham, who are entitled to all the benefits in his promises, leaving us unfulfilled.

And the mandatory duty for all the congregations in the filled churches all over the world is to win as many souls as each can win before our time passes. Try to fill your partnership position in the kingdom of the Father. Jesus, our high priest, did that by assigning the disciples to the churches and the people. Now the churches and us are more than enough to win the world for our Father. Do not be complacent on our own situation. As for me, I am saved. You are not done if you save only your family, your neighborhood, your city, and your society. You must also save the world. You will say, "How do I do that?" Get yours first, go to church to grow, read the Bible, and meditate with unceasing prayers to him for directions.

You are, in the first place, saved. Then fear of the Lord is your strong confidence. The Holy Spirit, who lives in you, is your counselor, companion, and comforter. Pray daily and ask him to take control of everything you do, including your evangelism anywhere, anytime.

The Holy Spirit gives directions to talk (what to say), to convict, to convince, and to convert the unbelievers. Being in the church for a while and being fed with the Word, plus your devotion and Bible reading, you already have knowledge. Therefore, you don't have to be afraid, not part of us. He gave us power, love, and a sound mind.

Having been conformed to the likeness of the Son, you are just going to impart to somebody whom the spirit will help to convict and carry on with the work from the inside of that new convert. After giving the tract or talking to them or the one, then lead them to believe with their hearts that Jesus is the Son of God and let them confess with their mouths that he died and rose again. Then get his or her name and phone number to include the name to the list of converts you are praying for every day till they get saved and comply. You will know this by calling from time to time either to know their church lives or if you are to take him to church if he is not far from you.

The beginning may seem hard, but we will soon get used to it. Sometimes you can get a speaker for your tract, or you can speak by yourself at a neighborhood and share your tract. If you don't have one, just preach mainly about salvation. Let them know nobody cares whether you go to hell or not. But Jesus cares, the Father in heaven cares, the Holy Spirit cares, the angels care in heaven, and Churches care as well toward you who is doing the conversion. All these are necessary because this country is of God's from the foundation, and Bibles were recognized even in schools, colleges, and universities, including Harvard.

The Bible was used as a science subject. Then what went on during the last centuries? And this seems to be overgrowing on what was laid with God. America really needs God back with us and concern with his right being what he wants from us for his love.

The fact is, so many things have gone wrong with the country that trusted in the Lord, turning back to trusting money and self-made happiness and ending in drinking, lesbianism, homosexuality, smoking, raping, kidnapping, and killing. The opposite of righteousness that the Father God taught us through the Bible is sin or unrighteousness. Whether you believe it or not, think about how we came to the world, think about the Israelites, and think about what the Bible is saying. Anytime we sin against him, there is a repercussion or rebuke.

Now also think about the creation, the discovery by the pilgrims who were able to stay and thank God as others have come and gone. And think of all the words proclaimed to honor God during the foundation of this great nation. Apart from that, think and ponder over how the spoken foundational words of their mouth have affected the country, drawing people to take shade under that biggest tree, like this very nation is the tree that everybody is coming to take shade. The favor here attracts the world to come to the country of immigrants.

The shade of many people come here to care for families; to have education to go back to; to help their countries in health, in legal matters, and in further education for the citizens; and many more further enhancements and developments. The world is learning from us like the apostle Paul, who did not come early but wrote more books in the Bible than all the other disciples. That's how God had made America as an example to the whole world. Though all nations are for God, America specifically put him first, earning us many blessings and making us the first world.

Too much blessings for a human being who is already variable makes him more variable. That is exactly what we are experiencing now as we deviate from all the directions we were thought to do as the very image of God and as the custodians of all his creations. We must be accountable to him when the time comes. Now we seem to be loving the world and being enemies to the one we should revere. Rather than causing a lot of abominations that only wreck the nation, I wonder if all the people in this world will maintain obedience from what is written in the good book, the Bible.

The baby boomers who did not get enough but wanted enough for their children and grandchildren who took things easy and are continuing to take easy things always want things the easy way. And too much of everything is bad. Therefore, balancing to get things done in the way the Creator wants means going through stages of conception of your destiny, then preparing for deliverance to maturity before being on a silver platter to wear the crown. Father Abraham, Joseph, David,

Hannah, and Jesus the Master all wore the cross before the crown. Going through any trials is only for a season; don't be deterred.

Those who usually go the easy way end up living in suffering due to lack of training. Hard ways make us mature and give experiences for a better tomorrow, which is supposed to be everyone's dream. And we should not rush to die fast as the youth these days are doing, dying with drugs and committing suicide, especially those whom we think have made a headway. So many things have gone wrong in America, the country that I, other individuals, and many nations love.

Let's examine some of the things that have gone wrong. Many countries in the world that like kidnapping (especially girls), killing (especially women), raping of women, killing of black males, and killing of police by retaliation from the black males all have to stop. Practicing homosexuality, lesbianism, transgenderism, and others also has to stop.

Are all these what the Father created us to do? No! These are of the opposition who made us his main target to do whatever he needs to do to thwart God's efforts and to make him, the devil, say, "Look at your stubborn children." And his mission is to accuse, a destroyer, because there are strings of punishment attached to all these sins and others for him.

Who he kills has committed the heaviest crime, and your hand is tainted with blood. Human blood from a tragic death is always crying for revenge. That person's blood, which is always crying for revenge, just like the blood of Abel against Cain, his brother, makes the Father angry, giving the heaviest punishment here on earth before you die and letting you go to hell in addition as your second death. Can we do all that it takes to end up in heaven?

Why are there kidnapping, raping girls, and killing women? A lot of women are ready to find someone to marry. Just tell her of your love, not kidnapping the children who have their lives way ahead of them. Their blood will cry to catch you for punishment. You were not born to kill but to win. The enemy, if you allow him, will let you lose your soul to hell with all kinds of sins, using your body to sin because he has no body, just a spirit. This is the country that kills more women than any country; about 65,000 die every year. Why, America?

Nobody was created with any sinful nature. But the accuser started luring Adam and Eve from the garden. Jesus redeemed us back to the Father, but the devil still pursues us here on earth, with his fallen angels, the demons. Witches, wizards, enchanters, sorcerers, and others use our bodies to sin. When you were young, someone you look up to like your father, mentor, coach, or even pastor did that to you, making you feel like it was a normal thing to continue to do to others, and now it is spreading against the will of Father God.

When America sneezes, the whole world coughs. Why? Because we are the world leaders. Because the whole world looks up to us due to so many sacrificial works we have done for the world and mankind, like a father taking care of his children, to win the heart of Father God. Anything that we do, the world will follow. All these things are growing not from before with our ancestors but mainly of late, mainly with Generation X, Y, and Z.

We would not have attained our blessings if they had performed so many sinful things like today. We wouldn't have gotten all these blessings. There might be some sin, but not to this volume. The baby boomers gave birth to Generation X and Y, and the jet age also gave birth to Generation Z. Computer technology came during their time, so to them, life should move very fast with full happiness. But everything that's too fast is not of God, who is full of patience.

Our chances are like what our parents have. No matter how deeply you offend them, they always forgive. If they can forgive, how much more the Ultimate One? The day before Oprah retired from the CBS show, she called all the men who were affected in that way when they were young, that someone might have used them for sex. About four hundred men attended just to speak out, to let it go. But how many were able to let it go away? Your mentor, your father, your pastor, or the man you looked up to and respected so much did that to you, and you think it is the right thing. Letting it go is not very easy.

It takes deliverance. The devil's invention to oppose the Father God out of his good works, is always in some; it might become part of them. And the devil, too, will get work to do. No wonder it is spreading to connect to their rights to be made as law now. So what about the Father's rights in the Bible? He is speaking through me for his rights versus the human rights of the evil one. Before we came here, he was here. We will go, and he will still be here. So whose rights matters? Can this kind of right give birth to children to fill the earth, like how we are about 6.4 to 7.5 billion on earth now? How many men can conceive and give birth? Considering the cost, what would the world be from the very beginning?

If you put wisdom into the creation, especially the anatomy, chemistry, physiology, and the like to create a human being, as custodians of all the beautiful things he had created and to be accountable to him, and now end up like sinful to be for the one who never created, but because of his stubbornness doing this to him and humanity, who came to steal, kill, and destroy always tormenting our lives. The fact is, God knew he is wicked and will not leave us alone. That is why he gave us the whole Bible to read and allow the Word to guide us. But with lack of knowledge, the people perished. Without learning the Bible, we will be vulnerable to him being constantly at war with Satan, our adversary, a great destroyer.

So many people have refused to acquire the knowledge of God to feed their spirit, soul, and body to live for him. And without that, we will be trapped by the enemy to live to satisfy the body by the evil spirit, using our bodies to sin. The way of creating our own happiness, which does not last, leads to short life and hell. The opposite way is living for the Holy Spirit's directions to go and meet Jesus in heaven since creating your own happiness in a sinful life is not the answer to worldly happiness.

Though those who are living as Christians for God are also being attacked in diverse ways, God got them covered. He knows the problem from the beginning and had already devised a way for them to stand up to it. The Father will never allow Satan to kill his children. Satan lets his children rise and gives them money for wealth but takes their soul in place to hell. Why not live in the way of the Lord, who created you and knows all about what you want and will give it to you at the appointed time? For his ways are simple and sweet to carry you heaven but would not be poor on earth too, if you only live in righteousness and love.

Stop thinking that you are smarter than he who created you and devising your own happiness and going in circles. The fact is, there can never be a world for us if there is no God. Among his numerous creations, just think about the earth, sun, moon, air, water, and oceans. Sin is "self interest now," which originated from Satan and his fallen angels, as I said, who uses human bodies to do things contrary to what the Father created, and blood is their food.

If someone you were looking up to like your Father, mentor, or friend did sex through your anus and you feel like continuing, it is not in the Bible; it is a sin. Just take a minute and think about the human sperm from man. A hundred drops of blood give one drop of sperm. Consider how many things you will eat to get that blood for that sperm. You can find out from doctors how difficult it's even to study about human beings. Very expensive sperm for conception to create people are going waste. A hundred drops of blood gives one drop of sperm.

See how doctors grow gray hair easily. That's the mystery they study. Then you put the most expensive spermatozoa on top of human excreta, the most useless thing from the body. Is this not debatable to the human world that this can create sickness and diseases? This needs a lot of brainstorming. This can also lead to hurting your partner. Hurting someone you love is against his rules, meaning we are not supposed to hurt but love.

Not that alone, it is killing your partner with time. Because the elasticity of the anus is not like the naturally created vagina, where a baby comes through and soon normalizes. Again, if you have been in a relationship that did not work, that can't be replaced with the same sex. Your past relationship did not work because you did not pray to get that one created especially for you, being a man or a woman. Pray for a bone of your bone, a flesh of your flesh, and blood of your blood long before you get married to locate one for you. That makes marriages as sweet as honey, being the marriage he ordained and had it waiting for you.

The Father created from your bone, flesh, and blood. And if you are a woman too, you did not take time to pray to get that man you were taking from his rib. He, in his infinite wisdom, has planned everything accordingly for our happiness. Because he enjoys our happiness and shares our sorrow, why the rush of running on our own wisdom and not reaching our destination and only dying unfulfilled? Your assumption of being created differently is originated by that twister to let the one you respect or look up to who did that to you make you think that it is normal. That was never normal. It is a complete deception.

That is the spirit that invokes you to do that and add riches to it to make you feel like you are on top of the world. Think about where you will go from here because you did not hook on to your Father for deliverance. Why are all the people not doing that? That spirit would not have chance to dwell in them and use them, which is already covered by the blood. Because we have accepted Jesus and he is covering us, not allowing the spirit to use us. You can do the same. It is never too late to get back on track to have salvation and to stop committing sin.

Yes, your rights have been amended by the authorities because you are also a human being. But where do you go from here, to hell or to heaven? That is the question you are to ask yourself if you are in this situation. The good news is, since he knew it is not your fault and have been trapped, he is also fighting to get you back to himself through Christians and pastors who are to act and act fast. The Father is ever ready to forgive you and bring you back to himself, just like how Jesus came to save mankind. Jesus left his teachings for us to continue his ministry as a church, awaiting his coming. Return to your Father.

Sins like killing, kidnapping, and raping can also run in families as their blood is running through you or your own innovation, being manipulated by the devil to kidnap women, raping, and killing them or be a serial killer. If you lose yourself by not going to church, this spirit would enter you to do the sin of his choice. That's why when you are caught, you wouldn't know what happened to you in the first place. That will be the spirit behind that sin, through you; to regret might be too late. Your Father can always forgive you, but since the devil has got a place in you, you will do the same sin again.

This can end up in stress or depression because the devil is at work in you with your soul, spirit, and body to kill you and to let you suffer with him, being a child of the Most High God, as he rebels against our heavenly Father. When this becomes obvious with you, then we need to go to church immediately to accept Jesus as our Lord and Savior and be liberated from this stronghold. No therapist, psychologist, or any medium can help us. We only need total deliverance in a church and be baptized by the pastors after completing basic Bible studies to be solidified in your stand in Jesus for spiritual strength.

When you become born again or get a new birth, the devil runs away from you because Jesus conquered him over two thousand years ago purposely for you and me. He is waiting for you to claim your victory that he conquered the devil for you. Why do you allow the devil to use you like he created you? He can't create a human being, but when God creates, he comes to steal your body and puff your shoulder high, like you are in charge of your world. The devil can make you rich (though you are in serious sin), make you refuse to come back to your Maker, and keep you in prison spiritually till you perish to be in his bank of fury fire.

Our owner is God. Having gained grip of you, the devil destroys you with no time till you are dead, making him win your soul to accompany him to the everlasting pit of fire that's awaiting him.

Even though he is tormenting the people who have accepted Jesus, Jesus makes use of his death. The blood of Jesus got us covered. Satan is jealous of us going to heaven, the Paradise, to be with the Father while he remains in the perpetual fire with his group.

The ways for his destruction are when you get money through his means, which might be consulting some mediums for directions, and you followed them. All the mediums are his agents, and he does not give the money or power for free but in exchange for your soul. With all the things you did on your own, you refused to seek coverage from Jesus or God. Then you resulted in drugs to kill you slowly. You ended up practicing homosexuality to die, or a friend might have convinced you to do that.

Chapter 7

The Enemy's Plan

Eventually of aids and wearing pull-ups because your anus can't hold your bowel movement. Knowing all the side effects but not having the willpower to stop is of the devil. This is not normal and has to stop.

One European came to my country of birth to play golf and took one of the guy who helped him and took him to Britain. That young man traveling was a blessing to the family. He was away for three years, and the man flew him home at his worst stage to come and die. The life of the twenty-five-year-old man was cut short by that man. Know that you are here on an assignment for the owner of this world to live and do what he has required of you to fulfill.

All churches are filled. Still, all clubs are also filled, and too much sins of abomination that make the Father angry are increasing. Due to the love he showed and blessed us. Living for the flesh instead of the spirit is what has gone wrong. The serious thing is how the world will follow us. So the earlier we think about His love and stay away from his dislikes and maintain all he is telling us in the Bible, the better. All is not lost yet. We can still turn back to make things up to him, for his love never ceases. There is none like Hm.

Things seem to be going the way God likes, and since he had created us in his image, he has a lot of patience for us to turn back like a prodigal son to receive the biggest party. Since you can never give up on your children, he will never ever pass us by, knowing our weaknesses. He has the patience to repent as an individual, as a people, and as a nation like America. Our Father is waiting for our repentance. We have been obedient to him in some areas that he is aware of. Therefore, America, no matter what has gone wrong, we can still return to our first love. He is calling his people back to him.

This is because during the foundation of good faith by our ancestors, asking for favor, grace, and blessing, Satan came to plant all these evils and abominations now going on in a nation so blessed like ours. So let's all become very serious with a prayer of redemption for him to redeem our country for us, though he doesn't want his children to compromise with sin. He still doesn't want to hold it against you to enable him to win you from his adversary, Satan, being the master sin orchestrator, never wanting happiness for God.

Almighty God, with his infinite wisdom, created the world, being heaven and earth, with his commands to be and then created all that are on earth on the fifth day. And on the sixth day, the three-in-one entity agreed to create man in his image to be the overseer of all that he had created on earth and be accountable to him, the Creator, but with his guidelines.

Before that, heaven was already in existence with God, who's seated with the angels. Lucifer was then the master for the praise and worship team. He was handsome and was called the bright morning star. He was dancing to appease God the Father. The only thing God can't do for himself is praise and worship, allowing people and all his creation to now do that, even mountains, trees, oceans, birds, and all his creation. He was loved and became very proud, when human being does it as the boss of all, now very proud to be equal to him.

For God loved Lucifer more with more closeness as he was always dancing and singing to make him happy and awarded him as the *bright morning star*. This awarded him some powers and chances from God, making him insolent to get the idea of sitting on the throne of God to be like God. This was a total disrespect to God for him to allow seraphim and cherubim to use some powerful sword to guide the throne of God. This led to a struggle by Lucifer, who wants to be like God to have the same powers. Almighty cast Lucifer down to earth. The heavenly Father said, "Woe betide the people on earth."

With this episode, Lucifer grew aggressive and was cast down with his supporting angels called the fallen angels, whom he was able to get to follow him to earth and in the oceans. God said, "Woe betide the people on earth." Since then, Lucifer now Satan, has become a serious enemy to man. God started to make man to replace Satan for his pleasure. The duty of Satan is to devise any sinful method to let man fall to prove to God that even the people he made to replace him are equally sinful just like him and to make God regret. He is anxious to never make the Father happy. It is like "If I fail, then everybody else should fail," being a very selfish, wicked individual.

Since time immemorial, he had been attacking our ancestors, Eve and Adam. He is so clever and has some powers because God did not stripped him of his powers, making him challenging Father God that his kingdom will be fuller than God's, thinking he is more powerful. He and his fallen angels with him, were the spirits like demons of various kinds that cause wars and accidents to drink the blood and other areas to only cause pain to humanity. Wizards and witches are also his agents. Being spirits, they dwell in the human body to sin and do nothing but let that body sin to pay the price with your soul and accompany him to hell. They normally feed themselves on human blood.

The result is just to make God feel the pain. Can you imagine that you have been taking time, wisdom, and pain to create something you cherish, like a human being, for your pleasure just for Satan, who has no idea whatsoever on your method of creation, to steal the body to use for himself and be led to death in destruction? This means Satan doesn't lose anything, but the Father loses something. Similarly, a mother who is pregnant with her baby for nine months gives birth to the baby and brings him or her up just to die one day—so premature. The pain will never go away.

It's just like how I lost my son at seventeen through an accident. I had him when I was seventeen years old, which interrupted my education. And losing him at the same age (seventeen) was a mystery caused by some of the devil's agents in the family. Many deaths have been caused by these agents of Satan that are assigned to various families, making him plant his agents in families and setups.

Another plan by Satan was when I was bitten by a snake. Being the youngest, I was in the middle of two girls. Immediately the Lord whispered to me to tie that foot, and I tied it three times to save myself from the snake poison, always planning to disrupt our God's given purpose.

Satan, knowing your agenda would be for God's glory, will be in a serious, constant war with you, using people around you as an agent to attack you with you not knowing what you have done. And God will keep an eye on you to protect you all along while you also pray and get close to him. Our adversary, Satan, and his agents never sleep unless they destroy someone.

That very day, we learned at school to tie our feet when we are bitten by a snake. I didn't see the snake but just felt like a pin hit my middle toe. I was only twelve years then, and we just arrived home, but within five minutes, I started perspiring. That was when I told them. They started crying while I was tying that foot about three times. Immediately my mom came from work with a taxi. She took me to the hospital, and the doctor was pleased that I tied my foot to save my own life. Still, I was serious in continuing my education while she was serious in interrupting me just to let me drop out. I was very serious in going to high school; here, we call it secondary school or high school. Friends lured me to parties; they have tried to for the whole vacation. Then one day, I agreed to go with them only to have them run away and leave me to my fate.

The result was me being pregnant. Even though I confided in her, she let me use some herbs, which rather made me pregnant. But I went back to school to complete my education anyway. When the boy reached the same age, seventeen, he died through an accident. She was very mean and hated my mom for loving me. My mom had the accident first, and I went to bring her with me. She was unfit to come. Later, as he came on vacation from high school, I sent him to bring her for Christmas only to have the same accident and died. Just to let you know, his roles against us runs in families too. Just balance this. You are not alone; he is really at work.

Try to explain how he dwells in people like witches to manipulate them. She was later found out to be an agent. Wow! As beautiful as she was? Along the line, things were happening. God was with me because things were happening to me seriously. The outstretched right hand will reach out to save me. And I will know as for this, it's some miraculous powers that brought me out. The devil is a master manipulator who changes his styles all the time. The only remedy is praying, using the Word with God's backing.

He promised to fight our battles for us to hold our peace. Father God has his agents, like Christians in the Bible believing in the churches. Also, pastors, apostles, evangelists, prophets, bishops, and righteous people are all agents of God. Whatever the Father does, Satan gets a duplicate copy and cuts in an evil way to show his powers to us. Being aware of this, Lord cautioned us not to lose our guard in fighting with wicked spirits and principalities in high places and that we mount our faith as a shield to cover our chest, get salvation as our helmet, equip truth around our loins, and shod our feet in the Word of God to prepare with the full armor of God to face the enemy's measles. That's to resist him to flee away from you. Knowing your right as a child of God will scare the devil away from you, just like how Jesus defeated him.

For us, we are covered inside out, so stay clean with Jesus and enjoy your heavenly right. With these few explanations, there are two entities in the world. There's the Father God Almighty, the Creator of heaven and earth and everything in it, and the Giver of all good and perfect gifts. Then there's one of the angels who turned against his Creator and imitated everything he does for evil, and his name is Satan, the accuser of the brothers, the tormentor of mankind, and the brain behind all painful, evil things and abominations in life, making us miserable.

You have the right to make your choice. The fact is, instead of choosing the Creator, we choose the creature. He could get you covered with the blood of his Son, Jesus, as the Holy Spirit also lives in you to counsel, comfort, and whisper wisdom and directions to us as a companion so as not to miss the right choices to make rightful decisions. Therefore, pray to make beneficial choices and make it up to the One who is more caring, loving, and forgiving than the wicked accuser who is waiting to share his suffering with us in the everlasting fire.

He is the originator of all sins of family trees—that our great-great-grandparents did, then our grandparents, and then our parents up to us. It is killing, raping, kidnapping, stealing, homosexuality, lesbianism, and all other sins. The devil shares them to the families to carry, so if one generation passes away, then the following one picks it up.

Oftentimes, one commits a crime and doesn't even know how he did it. It is the blood of the ancestors, which run through to follow up and keep committing that crime of serial killing and raping to keep the curse alive in that family. Therefore, different families have different curses. And that is what we call the ancestral curses or generational curses that rule in the family.

And it was Satan who manufactured all these sins that started from Adam and Eve in the Garden of Eden, just to play wicked for us to sin and hurt the Father God, whose only abomination is sin. This is making us disobedient, and oftentimes, no matter how he tries to forgive us and guide us with the Bible, many have no willpower to stop because that sinful blood is still boiling in them, only to face the consequences of punishment from God.

That is making human beings disrespectful to God the Father, making him regret for having created us in the first place. And Satan thought he is winning. In a way, I think he allowed Satan to exist among us for a purpose, or else we will be too pampered as spoiled children and refuse to live for God. Our sins will be prolonged more. He only knows all the roles and why, yet they all come with judgments. Just live your life right.

God is the Ultimate, the Supernatural, the Creator of the whole universe and everything in it, the I am that I am, the Supreme Orchestrator, El Shaddai, Jehovah Nissi, and all the attributes that I can call him; and Satan has none. He only wins our battles with the assistance of the very people he had created as beloved children and the partner for the kingdom's work. The annoyance is that Satan did not participate in the creation of anything good. He just causes the destruction of the very good things. The human beings that the heavenly Father created should be very smart and should resist Satan for him to flee from us with all his wickedness and plans.

To those who know that they do not have the willpower to try any sinful things, then desist from trying them in the first place. The fact is, not all of us have the ancestral cursed blood running through us for committing all those heinous sins, but we are trapped by evil friends to try or through modern gadgets like computers, TV, and media to see pornography and other things to practice sin. That gives the devil the power to invoke you to do more. Then stop sinning and start living righteously for the heavenly Father and build relationships. I mean healthy relationships of righteousness, the ones he commanded from the origin of his creation.

The righteous living for your salvation, which Jesus earned for us, allowed you to learn the Bible and get you to strengthen your relationship with God the Father who created us, with God the Son who came to our level to redeem us, and God the Holy Spirit who lives in us to help us in every area of our lives to live, to please God, and to make it to heaven. This is what is required of us children of God. Though some are so sinful beings, the agents of the devil are already entrapped to help the devil cause harm to those of us children of God who were created to replace him, Satan, at the time he turned stubborn and was thrown out.

There is a serious battle between the heavenly Father and his own creature, Satan, who rebelled. The churches and Christians, pastors, preachers, evangelists, bishops, and prophets are standing as soldiers to fight this battle with the soldiers of Satan, like demons, wicked spirits under the sea, territorial spirits under the earth, wizards, witches, occultism, and the like who fight for Satan. This is a fight between God and his creature.

They form the fallen angels who fell with the then Lucifer, who was so handsome to be called the bright morning star but rebelled and became Satan and was cast down unto the earth. God did not snatch the powers he gave to him, so he is backing his agents. The Ultimate even started backing his beloved children from the Garden of Eden when they have fallen. And as a result, Jesus came. When he left, the Holy Spirit also came to be in everybody and at every place at the same time. The Father, who knew the ending from the beginning, knew all these and provided all the solutions before they even came.

The battle is great and tense, but we are born to win. And winning depends on how smart we are to renew our minds and hook on to God and His word as our defense. How can a pot fight with the Potter? The battle of the Creator versus Satan had already defeated him over two thousand years ago, but he never gives up because of shame and refuses to accept defeat. Beloved, the battle is tough, but it is of the Lord's, so let's fight and win.

To win this battle, we are to humbly submit to prayers, fasting, and studying of the Word to empower ourselves with our salvation, faith, truth, and the Word of God to energize us like soldiers. When we do that, we become spiritually strong to be able to win this battle, for the Father is behind us to defeat the enemy who is tormenting us in this world. The expectation of the enemy who is also an enemy to our Father is to see us not enjoy this life, not be happy, not even laugh, and not have happiness in any marriage.

Marriage, being the first institution that he created for union, for reproduction, and for intercession to support his glory, was the very first thing that the enemy attacked and is still attacked in diverse ways. Women, whom God had specially taken his time to create with curves made so beautifully to appease men, have their precious parts showing to the public. How shocking and horrible it is to see sex shown openly to people, reducing women's precious image, and it is especially created for men. Women need to be treated special.

The most depreciating dignities and unsuccessful relationships with men and women have given birth to homosexuality, transgenderism, and all the things that God abhors seriously. When sin knocks at your door, beloved, try to run away. Sin is feeding the flesh and is satisfying the things in the world. While holiness and righteousness feed the Holy Spirit in us to appease God, the Holy One and Mighty One compare to none. Relationship issues are crowing the devil's world now with horrible things that never happened in the past, only in the current.

When the angels of God went to burn Sodom and Gomorrah, Lot sheltered the angels, and the men went to Lot to release them to have sex with them. He pleaded with them to take his virgin daughters instead. Then suddenly, the men became blind. The whole city of Sodom and Gomorrah were burned to ashes with the people and everything. That is how serious God hates this sin of abomination, demoting his creation he so much values.

Why are transgenders only in this country so much? Who is wiser than the Creator himself to create a man in a woman's body or a woman in a man's body? These are all from Satan, who is always trying to duplicate all the good works of the Father, whom he rebelled against. Satan uses people's bodies for awkward things to sin against him and get the chance to put us in trouble, making our minds the battlefield where he plays with our feelings and thoughts, if we allow him. Studying the Bible will give you knowledge and words to discipline him and to avoid his kind of practices.

The only difference is that a boy can resemble the mother and look like a woman. On the other hand, a girl can also resemble the father. But this doesn't change your gender. The two DNAs formed us, so we are to take after one of our parents to show who gave birth to us. The trouble of being in the everlasting fire (to make God lose his good works) is very painful and threatening against mankind. One can take resemblance of both the mother and the father.

Nobody has any feelings like Him in the whole world for his children. Only the mother's love comes a little closer. We are so blessed that we are leading the world. When Satan gets us here, he gets the whole world as followers. It becomes like a parasite until we lose our guard and leave people who have been blindfolded the way the devil wants us to live, and it's going on right now. The enemy should not win. We have been created by the highest power, redeemed by the highest love, and the most powerful spirit lives in us. Therefore, we should not be alarmed but fight Satan consistently till we win and avoid his ways.

One most important thing we are to do is to yield and depend on the Father in all that we do in our lives to please him; agree to the teachings of our Savior, the Messiah, Jesus; and meditate on the Word to empower the Holy Spirit in us. Then we confirm that we are more than conquerors.

He created us and lives in us, which makes him greater than the devil and his agents who are in the world. Make sure to make good choices that the devil cannot win against. He never gives up on us. We should also continue to resist him and to flee if he comes a thousand times. Using the Word as our weapon to combat the enemy, if you know you're right, he is not so fearful. Your Father in heaven has got you covered twenty-four seven anywhere, anytime in all battles in this wild world.

Nothing about the devil is good or beautiful. He invokes our bodies if we do not resist him strongly with the word and with righteousness. He invokes the body to kill, rape, kidnap, steal, and be greedy, practicing abominable sins and more of the very sin that collapsed Sodom and Gomorrah. He makes you think that you are in a man's body or in a woman's body, just to confuse and disgrace you to give pains to your Father God, who created you that way to be happy. He knows better than all on earth, for nobody is like him, and no one can create like him.

Then why do you have to be unhappy and trade your heritage? You're a father figure, walking your daughters to their weddings, and you're now eating alone and feeling lonely. You see what the enemy can do? He came to dwell in your body and puffed you up to be you without the owner to disgrace yourself. He tears your precious family apart without the head. Your grace now has turned to be a disgrace. Just weigh this: Where are your children now? They are shy to come closer.

Imagine holding your daughter's hands on the aisle to be married and sitting at the table head to listen and give advice to solve family problems. Now she is a woman, one who is glorious and befitting. See how he has made his children fatherless to their face and shock. They have broken apart, can't even come closer anymore. This is the kind of disgrace that the devil wants for us and makes you feel you are on top of the world. The heavenly Father is grieving, having created us in His image in the first place, and the devil is laughing at both of us. Our choices can make us and the Father win. It's never too late to renew our minds to live solely for the Father, who knows what's best and wants to feel proud of us instead of grieve.

Chapter 8

The Father's Wrath

It's just like parents to feel proud when things in life are going on naturally for the children—the daughter or son got a good career, a good job, and a good marriage; bought a beautiful house; and have obedient and beautiful children. That's when the parents celebrate their children with all those great things mentioned. That was why parents send children to Churches, and Sunday schools to follow the steps of righteousness and to make it to God to overcome the world with those qualities. No parent is proud of a child bringing stigma to the family and putting that family to shame, knowing well that is against the Father's will, which must be obeyed.

A typical example would be our Maker expressing here through Jesus and through the Bible: "Do all the sayings in the Bible rely on me 100 percent? When you get what you will eat for today, don't worry about tomorrow. Leave tomorrow to me. I will always make sure you have enough for the day. If I care for the birds in the air and the flowers in the garden, how much more you, human being, my own image, whose hair I know the numbers of? That shows how seriously I care about you. It's a very live simple logic. Live right, and make it up to me to make sure your destinies are fulfilled regardless of the enemy's traps, which you have already overcome in the world since being with me. Then live without fears but with love for one another."

That is all that is required of us. Not the greedy and wild lifestyles with attitudes. Some search for other powers like occultism, controlling the new world for power on earth and trading your souls for hell. Take note of that. Why do you die for your adversary who hates you and wants nothing good for you? Think twice and renew your mind. All power belongs to the Mighty One. I am begging the men to be careful since they are always the power pack. Women are rather the vulnerable ones and are not so much into powers.

Sin (self-interest now) is one thing that turns God away from us. Though he sent Jesus to heal us so that we can come closer to him, still our brother, the accuser, will not give us any chance. Satan's only works is to make sure you sin so that you can't get closer to your Father, who has given you a chance to call him Daddy. That is Abba Father showing how much he loves you. He allowed Jesus to become our brother to live with us. He felt our pains so that he can teach us how to live for our beloved Father who is in heaven and is preparing for his kingdom to come on earth.

The advocator's, knowing that God is all-powerful and all-knowing, is always giving and devising combats to Satan's tricks from luring us into sin constantly to lose our mercy, our loving kindness, our protection, our deliverance, our favor, and all those things in store for us to prove his love to us due to our stubbornness. So how can some be obedient to the teachings in the Bible that Jesus taught us who are still seeking for sin and some be obedient?

Still there are many good things with the Father, who doesn't want to lose you and me to the one who did not know how to create a human being or anything and only knows how to destroy. He makes a way for people to meet you and witness you and meet you and give you tracts, telling you how to repent and that your Father needs you and doesn't want you to end up in hell. So don't harden your heart and yield to him, for the time is getting shorter and shorter. Pastors are preaching on television shows like Trinity Broadcasting, Daystar, and many others, giving clear indications that you can't keep on continuing to live in constant sin. You can't deny Him, did not know or hear anything about God. It's all over the earth.

Christmas and Easter—which celebrate Jesus's birth, death, and resurrection—should let you know better that though he forgives and gives many second chances, he has also zero tolerance for sins. That was why he said, "If my people will turn to me with all their hearts and pray for forgiveness, I will forgive them and heal their land." Our nation needs a total healing now for turning away from God, for even blessing us so much. All indication of all that Mother Nature is showing are signs of God's wraths that tell us to repent and come back to him and run away from sin.

So how many times are we not recognizing God's interest first but our sinfulness and being pretenders, which show great disrespect? Our hands are full of sin and are tainted with blood for killing one another and committing suicides. Taking your like to run away from trouble means going to hell. Repenting, receiving Jesus, and living to fulfill your life is the answer.

The signs of God's wrath are tornadoes, twisters, earth slides, hurricanes, earthquakes, and others. All that we know to do is to rebuild. Why not stop sinning and preventing them from happening frequently in the first place? If he created us in his image, this means he lives in us and will do things he does if only we will follow his commandments and statutes. He allows all good things to happen and prevent all bad things from happening. Every good and perfect gift is from the Son, the Father, and the Holy Spirit. Nobody performs like him.

The Trinity can do all things, beloved. Let's start doing what is required of us to cool his heart and stop Mother Nature's disastrous destructions. Let's be mindful that Jesus came to die to save us with his precious blood and take us away from sin. We were led astray, and he reconciled us back to God by his grace and not by our works because we are still in sin. We can be free from sin to enjoy this right continuously till we meet him again.

He paid that expensive price of death by crucifixion; I don't know how many people could do this for our own children. Then we were cleansed and sanctified to living in righteousness, which is crucial for our continuous salvation, taking us to heaven to meet him. See the love he displayed. He even called us his friend, and those of us who will get the chance to join him in the world to come will become coheirs and reign with him in the kingdom.

All the things that are happening here in America are more than those happening in other countries. Once in a while, they happen elsewhere. They are also sinful nations around the world but not as enormous as ours. America's sins are enormous, and we are leaders to many countries, if not all, which had earned us the first country. If we refrain from it, many nations will also refrain. If we continue, they will also continue as they are ringleaders.

We were chosen as leaders by the Creator. Since all our good things have affected other nations, our evil things also affected them. This is really hurting God, but he loves his children. And if we can make it up to him, all these causes of Mother Nature's calamities can be minimized or even stopped. Until I came here, I haven't heard about certain things like them in my home country. As a baby boomer, only twice have I heard of some slight earthquake without any major damage. That doesn't sin. But our sins are caused by the majority that affects the whole world. God is grieving for this great country.

Whenever God blesses us so greatly, the result becomes ungratefulness. Just like Solomon who asked for wisdom and God gave him wisdom plus many blessings, he ended up marrying so many women from neighboring countries and worshipping various gods against God's will. So, like America, after God has made us the first country for acting as such, now we are doing things that he abhors (mostly), like challenging his wisdom of creation as if he did not know the right things to do, making him grieve, and making us seem smarter than him. Can the pot say it is greater or smarter than the potter? Incredible. Let's ponder properly.

How many times do we have to offend him for having created mankind? From the Tower of Babel that was being built to reach heaven to Noah's time with the flood of forty days and forty nights, which led Noah to make a sacrifice of thanksgiving and the aroma led him to show the rainbow that no rain like that ever will come to spoil the world. That alone shows his love for us as perishable human beings, and that is awesome. Eve, too, led Adam to grieve for him from the onset. Still he is following us every step of the way, not giving up on us.

Yet still these mentioned practices caused the fire in the then Sodom and Gomorrah. Even the angels assigned to cause this fire, the people before that wanted to have sex with them, the angels, instead of Lots virgin daughters. They were blinded by the power of God through the angels. That shows how he abhors that homosexual sin. Can you please read the Bible to advise yourself? Refer to Leviticus 18:22–30 and 1 Corinthians 6:9–20.

If these practices are acceptable to God, why would fire destroy Sodom and Gomorrah? And why was blindness given to males who wanted to sleep with the angels? Who can brainstorm and see that the human he had taken time to create would put the most expensive blood to the most inferior feces or human excreta to even cause harm to the neighbor's anus? That can cause sickness to him. Do we love one another? No!

Only the devil can make us to think these are the right things to do. The enemy is envious of our preciousness and only leads us to disgrace. Your so-called male wife feces now come unannounced that they are to put on diapers, why God didn't make this from His creation?

A golfer took a youth to molest him in my home country and returned him like that, killing him slowly and adopting innocent children to be trained in that category. That child, whom the family thought would be taken care of, ended up getting sick with toilet coming unannounced, then the man left him to come and die in his country. So what category does that individual belong to? A human being or a monster?

The Bible tells us how his chosen people also grieved to him several times for their deliverance from Egypt to the Promised Land. Several times back and forth led the forty-day journey took a whole forty years due to their disobedience and stubbornness. Know that we are nothing without him. The enemy really has an agenda to fulfill, which is to humiliate us every step of the way, and we should be aware of that by now.

Not making us God's children is ridiculous as his Spirit lives in us. When shall human beings learn? Can we access the mystery of birth alone to stop us from sinning against him and stop grieving to our Father in heaven? If we do not stay away from such things, he will allow more serious things to happen to us. We think we are smarter and stronger when we rebuild each time Mother Nature strikes. What about our lives? Don't our lives also matter to us since we lose human beings too, apart from houses and others?

These are all the innovations of Satan to let God be aware that the people he created to replace him are equally as bad as he is. There's so much grieving, not thinking about how he gets the chances to accuse you and to let your sin rebound back to you and leave you suffering. When parents see their children messing up their lives with drugs, prostitution, and others, how do they feel? They would feel embarrassed and depressed or whatever. God's feelings are more than that.

But if human beings feel that, what about the one who knows better than us, his creatures? Sin leads us to a series of suffering, ending up with the one who rebelled against him. The punishment for the devil is coming back to hit us, beloved children, like many have suffered. He will do anything if they seek him to escape this punishment. By ending up in hell, the perpetual place with him. the people he created to replace him. Those in the abomination, which is clear that he had forbidden us, without reading the Bible and going to churches, as they are constantly echoing unto us, there will be no excuse again.

God, who loves his children, forgives and gives second chances for knowing the plans and our frame, waiting for us to repent and come to reason with him, no matter how grievous the sin we commit is, just like the prodigal son. The father was so happy that he threw him the biggest party. Folks, nothing is too late for us to renew our minds and turn from homosexuality, lesbianism, and others and return to our Father, who never refrains from loving us. His love is unconditional and perpetual by the grace of the blood of Jesus as our right.

That is one thing we can't wait too long for. The clock is ticking, and our interest now is rising, which is continuous, like nobody knows what is going on. Many are naive, living dead in the world. The good shepherd came to die for sins and brought us to reconcile with the Father, who is our big owner. Dying to sin means sin should totally go away by our effort because that accuser will not rest unless he causes some harm to us by his everyday plan, which is roaring like a lion, wanting someone to devour. And we do not have to lose guard but equip ourselves with all that the Father is telling us.

He gets flared up when all things seem to be taken for granted and when all avenues seem exhausted. He gives the chance to caution us using Mother Nature to show us that he is getting furious and that we should not lose our guard of reaching the peak of the sin ladder as our country is the leader of the world. God becomes sad, just like when we are hurt and become sad. When someone you love hurts you, you wouldn't want to be hurt, but it is natural to us, human beings, as we take from him. How do we live and avoid his wrath?

What is happening here, like Mother Nature's disasters, reminds us to be awake and to stop. I mean to try and live away from sin, though we are living in sin with our carnal minds in the world, making Jesus come and pay that price to redeem us and die with our sins. Why should we still stay in sin?

Unless we make use of his death by denouncing sin, getting salvation to lead us to eternal life, we will always be trapped by the enemy through the carnal mind, thinking we are smart. How can a creature be smarter than the Creator? It's very simple logic, and he asks us who we are mocking. Each one will reap all that he or she has sown at the Judgment Day. Your good works will send you to heaven, while your disobedience and stiff neck will send you to hell.

We are sinful, but he is mindful of us, and he cares, loves, and finds a way to redeem us. Since he knew the end from the beginning, he had already put measures in place to free us by his grace and not our works. The significance of salvation allows the Holy Spirit, who replaced Jesus, to become our intercessor, counselor, comforter, and companion who tries to convict, convince, and convert us by living in us. The Holy Spirit helps to quicken us and fight all the battles of the enemy and our adversary—Satan, the devil; all his fallen angels; the worldly agents like those in the seas and rivers; and demons, witches, and wizards who mainly use human bodies to kill and drink their blood and to commit you to their side. Their food is drinking blood.

With this, the Bible is there to guide us to resist and oppose him anytime he comes, to flee away from him. He doesn't rest unless he causes harm to someone. The Father doesn't want him and his agents—like the fallen angels who are the demons, witches, and wizards—to harm us, and the Father, too, doesn't sleep or slumber. We are also to put on the armor of God to challenge him. And until we read the Bible to equip ourselves, we will not have any weapon to fight him. He is a fearless fighter unless you read the Bible to discipline him.

Those weapons to fight are the truth, the breastplate of integrity, and the right standing with God. Then the good news will prepare us for our salvation, plus our faith will destabilize all his tricks, and his pokes will come to naught. Lack of knowledge, only to go in circles by your own power and cause blunders against the Father, will arouse his wrath and make the enemy very happy. The devil will be happy that we are finally going to be the culprit and suffer for our lack of knowledge. Taking the time to find out the answers will let us be defeated even before the Judgment Day comes. Make no mistake; the Father is surely going to come and judge us.

Therefore, take note of what the signs of Mother Nature are telling us—that the end is approaching. We are to repent from all sins. We are not to be taken by surprise into the lake of fire. This encourages us to be on the same page with Jesus, the Proud Purchaser, to complete the coverage he won for us over two thousand years ago. There's no reason to allow that to go to waste. Just settle things with him by stopping the fury of Mother Nature. They are so intense here than any other nation. Many nations have followed our example as a leader.

This is because our sins are also intense. Yet he always forgives us and loves to reason with us. He is a forgiving and loving Father. He caused flood by making it rain for forty days and forty nights in the days of Noah. After the flood had receded, Noah made a sacrifice on an altar for God, and the aroma reached him and made him regret about the flood and promised that never again would he make that kind of punishment. He regretted and promised that never again will he use flood to destroy mankind, using the rainbow as a reminder never to spoil the world and humanity with flood ever again. Check, how he loves to reason with consideration.

Many among us do not sin consciously and really love him with all our hearts, and many are Christians or unbelievers but can't discern wrong from right or want to go to church for salvation, baptism, and righteousness as preparation for eternity.

These are our weapons to draw our brothers and sisters to also love him. For many are out of ignorance or naivety, or the world is too much for them. The world really is too much for all of us unless you totally surrender to the One, who is your Owner. Nothing comes as rosy or on a silver platter. We can't just live for the sake of living, like we are hanging on and just eating, sleeping, having sex for reproduction to fill the earth and dominate, and partying. It's happiness all the time; if not, suicide. Suicide takes you straight to hell. Your life is not for you to end. He who gives has the right to take it, awaiting judgment. Money, too, is not the answer; sometimes it can't even heal you.

Living by compliance with everything about him and why we are here gives firm foundation. He is doing all that it takes according to his planning for us, which is not of evil but of good, which is comfortable and an expected end for us. He is making all things work for our good. Because when we are born of him, then we overcome the world from dangers. Since the Holy Spirit lives in us and is greater than all that is in the world, conforming to his measures doesn't lead us to live in the world with any sort of rigidness while striving for greatness but all by him.

Chapter 9

The Revelation

The pains toward how human beings are not listening and adhering to what the Creator is telling us but putting more premium on what is in the world many times became more sorrowful, and sometimes I cried when compared to what the Bible is telling us. All this while, I thought it was me loving, reverencing, and leaning on him more and appreciating all he has done for me and my children. Despite how my marriage ended, where we are right now, is all from Him; in him, we live and have our being. All are full of miracles along.

We all ended up in the United States. The result was forgiving him, taking care of him on his sickbed, and giving him the last respect—a fitting burial and a nice tomb—without seeing the new wife who left him on his sickbed. The three oldest children came to the funeral but paid no cost and left all the contributions on us while they were with him. He was a money-conscious man too. Worshipping God and money is like serving two masters. And forgiveness freed our minds and hearts to heal us, and blessings from our heavenly Father are always true for forgiveness and others.

Though I made some mistakes, I can recall my childhood. When I became a born again in 1988, I felt awful in doing some things I didn't know were wrong and shouldn't have done to hurt my Maker, and I quickly repented. Since then, I make sure to do the right thing and confess daily for any sins of commission or omission—these are those sins I did knowingly and those I did unknowingly. Confess daily for forgiveness, and make sure nothing sinful will be left in blocking you from reaching out to God. Sin is the only major hindrance.

From that day in 2014 in the past, there has been a major acceptance of this community of gays and lesbians against the Father's wish. I loved and respected this man so much, but I cried for having chosen a human being over God is an abomination. And the follow-up also came to confirm it. Since then, there has been a revelation from God on how he is grieving because the very people he created for his pleasure are now becoming a pain for him through Satan.

Then this became obvious, and I am always with tears and dates whenever I get the discernment from him, telling me to go ahead and write this book and preach against it. That is the meaning I am writing. He will be telling me what to write. All are about the deliverance of the people in that kind of practice and others that will prevent us from going to heaven.

Jesus is not here yet because a lot more people are going to hell with Satan to make his death on the cross unprofitable. This painful death, is it going to benefit my people? This is the question he is constantly asking. "If the people I have created will repent and humble themselves before me, I will hear them and heal their land." He will love to hear us coming back from sin to make it up to him. There is nothing he wouldn't do for us, his beloved.

Since then, whenever there is anything going on, he starts discerning to me, like telling me how he felt so sad with the way he had been treated regardless of the love he is showing us. And my answer was to cry and pray how mankind can make it up to him, to find peace here on earth and in heaven. I will be quoting some of the dates and times that I was able to write them down. Whenever I start, they go, like someone is dictating to me. I was writing my life story book before He stopped me to write this one to his beloved children, see how He cares.

This is so that many people could read apart from the church outreach, which I sometimes do to myself. As I said before, if all the pews filled with Christians take upon themselves to win as many souls as they can in a day, a week, or continuously till they are able to convince more souls, it will enable us to meet Jesus, who is coming soon. The Father's concern is how so many people are going to go to hell if he comes now. Haven't we got ears to hear or eyes to read the Bible? What is wrong with many of us, being naive like nothing really is going to happen and like we are brought here to eat, to party, and to produce babies, then when we die? Is that the end? Where do we go from here? We need to find answers ourselves on where we go from here from reading the Bible. Going to Church too will help us.

Still, the time for his coming is long overdue. Whether we prepare or not to meet Jesus, one day he will be becoming like a thief, and that will be the end. Losing focus and forgetting he will come someday with his judgments, are ours to decide, yet that is reality. He started talking to me frequently, those days and he said, "You better put them into writing for many people to get access to read." I pray that this book reaches as many people as possible to read and take note that if perishable human beings would know better to find out about life after death, it will be good for us. And we are to be curious than insisting on our rights that contradicts the rights of God.

Then the right of the Supreme Super Supreme, who has no ending and beginning, the Alpha and Omega who created the heavens and the earth and everything it contains and made us custodians. God made us in his image, but a little lower than the angels who watches over us. Whose right should we accord? His right should be first and foremost. He should be obeyed first before anyone. No man should be chosen over him. That will be serious.

Oftentimes, human beings forget that even when a tree is cut down, it will grow again. But we die here as we are even just passing by. He existed before we got here, and when we will leave him here, he will still be here. Our purpose here will come to an end one day. Heaven or hell will be our destination, being schooled for one of them in our journey.

We owe Him our lives. The planet that we live on is His. The air we breathe, the water, and all things we survive on come from him. Why can't his peace be our peace and his likeness be our likeness? After all, we are His image. Let's talk about relationship theory and how our Father created us in his image to replace the then Lucifer, who was amusing him and turned stubborn and fell together with some fallen angels, the demons working for Lucifer, now Satan.

We are to take his place and reason with the Father as he has given us all the guidelines in the Bible to guide you and me. So, why majority of us are following this fellow named Satan? On August 10, 2014, at 5:00 a.m. on Sunday, he prompted me and whispered, "My daughter, start praying for the gay community for the Holy Spirit to convict, convince, and convert them to Me. They are mine, and the enemy has taken them as captives to practice that. See how wonderful they were all made. Pray for them all to stop practices including lesbianism and becoming a transgender. None of them is written to be practiced in my good book, and all are abominations. You know they are so precious and valuable to me that I don't want them to go to hell with the enemy. And they have been redeemed by the most expensive blood and precious Son and are still making no use of this blood."

On August 16, 2014, at 5:00 p.m., I was hearing the Father, "I am more than ready to heal my own children from this dirty game. If only they will listen, convert, and seek Me, I will make them brand-new that they will not know they were the same people. Write them in the book as I keep on telling you all the methods I put together to form them and even the mystery of birth.

"Are they aware that God celebrates their births with their first cry in the world? Because they are precious in my eyes and they are costly too. Those practices demote and devalue the price I put on them. All that the devil has put them through will be a thing of the past. I am their Father God, and I am aware of what they have gone through and will never stop being aware of what they have gone through and will never stop fighting for them.

"They would be liberated through the grace of the blood still pleading for them. Jesus, my Son, came for those who are sick and those who are not well. They do not need any doctor. They will be healed from all the abominable sins, which is like a parasite eating their body to destruction." Check how beautiful and handsome you were created to be involved in this shameful act to disgrace God and his creation. See, God made all his creations beautiful.

He continued, "The first ministry I created was marriage, which was for union, fellowship, and multiplying to replenish the earth and for my pleasure. Seeing this, Satan turned into a snake to convince Eve to get Adam to have both commit sin. Though they were driven, I didn't leave them alone. I sent Jesus to come and redeem them. And still he is chasing them.

"Lucifer lost his position and was driven unto the earth. Know that I love you and forgive you, yet no sin goes unpunished even before I consider forgiveness. I chastise and punish you as my children for you to grow to maturity and to make you refrain from sin. Still you have forgotten Sodom and Gomorrah and are doing this. When will you ever learn? Or have you never heard anything from the Bible or the church at all? Or are you just closing your ears and eyes to the truth?

"The people I have chosen—where you can see me through them too—my creatures, have chosen over me. Why? It might be from the pressure of the obstructionist from their opponent who is defusing their agendas and forcing them to get others' support and chose them over me. Or what? If they love the people, they should be concerned about where they go from here. The leaders fight for their mortal comfort here on earth. What about the immortal comfort in heaven? If the opponent played a part like what I am expressing, they will also have their share from the leader who is coming. They will see things for themselves and miss the old president just to be deceived by "Had we known, I would have not discriminated."

Your Creator abhors all sins. The taking of human lives, transgenderism, homosexuality, killing, raping, and the like make him grieve and make him regret creating us humans in his image. Because we are his image and there is no way we should do anything like this, why are we doing them? Let's continue another time as tears flowed from your eyes. My sorrows and pains had affected you to cry for me. Since then, writing this book became obvious, and the devil also intensified his grip on me and expanded my problems and distractions to delay this book. I have changed three computers for this book.

This book was started in 2014 just as, and since then, I had been battling on the property he gave to my children in court. Litigation started on the share of the properties we both had shared during the divorce case over three decades ago. Then he declared bankruptcy and got sick, and our children and I consented and allowed him to occupy the house where he died. And this brought some litigation by my stepchildren to sell the house which I have been holding the trustee for them. Without any of them having any documents, they have paid the judge to sell that house. The documents are intact with me; I have them. The distraction, being my great pain, was the fact that my leniency has become my stupidity, for the man whom I made a fortune with went to someone else and dumped me. Moving here for the children's sake, I had to give him help as forgiveness, which landed me in this pain and problem, costing me a fortune for a long-time litigation.

Loving God even when he is hurting, I had to also love my neighbor like God loves us. Writing this book now, I had to work and pay for lawyers back in my home country. And the judges get bribes without looking at our documents because of injustice stomach. When the house was in court, I could not even concentrate and write faster. Whenever I am writing, it is like he is next to me to tell me what to write. Completion will be my gain and relief as I am speeding up to complete this.

On August 19, 2014, at 2:30–3:00 p.m., one pastor in my home country got the revelation and called to tell me how God wants to use me. That was why he brought me to this country, but I have not been located. He had wanted me to be discovered in the political arena to enable him to talk to them through me due to the way he loves this country as their ancestors included him in the foundation to make it solid. And I don't know what to do. All the letters I wrote to talk to somebody did not yield any result to let them know that God is mindful of this country and wants to be in their midst. Even though I have written letters to some of them, they didn't reach anywhere to get any attention.

I was constantly praying with the online prayer line, and the bishop was also constantly prophesying someone is about to assume a new position from June, July, and August, so get ready. And I know it was me. And so I tried to talk to the president and wrote a letter, which I did later, and I wrote to the then secretary and to the Clinton Foundation. And all to no avail. I still have all my copies intact. No reply came since then.

The devil knows my love for God has been tormenting me since my youth. I have really gone through a lot. But each time, the all-knowing Father brings me out. This is being written no matter what the devil does. So many sins are capital sins, and they are not pardonable unless you take notice to repent, fast, and pray for forgiveness. Knowing what the result will be, I was trying to prevent it. I did my best, and it was not enough with the devil's obstructions. The outcome is on the table now as we experience what seems like a dream.

Homosexuality, lesbianism, transgenderism, killing, and raping, among others, are those that are being greatly practiced here; and he is employing you to refrain from them all as he considers them very heinous sins. Stopping them will stop him from grieving and will rather make him feel comfortable. Because he is saying to himself that we are the people he created in his image and gave us his unconditional love plus all the beautiful creations and made us custodians.

I started writing these down on June 7, 2014; the regular time to pray with my prayer line was ten thirty to twelve thirty. I opened my phone and fell asleep. I was prompted to wake up at exactly 1:00 a.m. and heard the gentle voice. I listened and took notes as I had refused them other times. He said, and I quote, "We need to mount a platform or a talk and advocate and show and tell my people all over the world to stop their sin, especially all the abominable sins that I abhor so badly and led to the ruin of Sodom and Gomorrah and took my beloved people from me. Satan is still on the move, and I have to see to stop them from this world.

"The churches representing me are not sounding the alarm very seriously and loudly to the Christians to carry them home to the unbelievers. This kind of attitude and lifestyle is growing rapidly and is grieving me as your heavenly Father never envisages this will come up again after burning Sodom and Gomorrah. Lucifer, and kater Satan, has really been very stubborn to Me, using the people whom I had created to take his place. Echoing to them seriously and rapidly through talk shows plus the books can make some difference.

"Therefore, jot them down and compile them for the book. I am always here to remind you. I know how you cry for Me, and your tears are not dropping on the floor. So we have to do it in any way possible to let the people know My grieving."

He explained, "Talking about the relationship theory, I created you in my image, and you are supposed to do what I am doing and not contrary to my way of living, though I have been doing my best to cover you from the devil, who was the most handsome Lucifer who turned against me and was driven from heaven with his fallen angels. He is now operating as the evil within human bodies only to sin against Me since I created you to replace him when he fell from heaven to the earth.

"That was why he attacked the first institution I created as man and wife, Adam and Eve, to take leisure with them like what I was doing with him before he turned stubborn. You have been his target even from the womb, knowing this day will come that I will use you. And you know how many times he had attacked but had not been able to consume you due to my protections." Now, negatively, he is trying to turn man to man, and woman to woman.

I was to complete this book before President Barack Obama leaves the White House on January 20, 2017, but I had a lot of distractions that had been heavy on me, and I had been on and off for all this while. I wanted some assistance from the one I am writing for and even wrote to him from the beginning of the year for help for him to move faster. But I did not get any response, not knowing if he received the letter. Or it might be later or never. Still I had no choice but to write regardless of what is going on. I left my own life story book to write this as I was asked to do exactly that with his directions. That will enable him to include on his foundation.

Now President has left the White House. If he will find me to listen to do this as his foundation to take it up to the Father, what he wanted him to do to His way and reverse things to bring those involved to obey the commandments and escape the rapture, that would be very great to Father God, and all will be forgiven. That makes the people in line to obey God.

Though he is a Democrat and Liberal, no president has ever given more rooms like this. He means his time to the extent of becoming the law of the country. That is the reason God wants us to pray for our leaders for directions. Being chosen by God to lead, entails a lot of directions through prayers from the people that he is leading. All leaders need prayers to do the right thing to represent God to His people, unless dictators do their own dictatorship to please themselves and not the people they represent. Why do you think the past presidents couldn't do this—like promoting things that go against God?

Why do you think the past presidents couldn't do this? Though he did so many great things and fought so hard for the people, this seemed to overshadow things and dissuade the Evangelicals and many Christians away from him. Even though many loved him, we were shocked of that approval and were confused. In everything, choose God first. He alone can make everything possible for our goodness. One painful thing we are doing against God through the devil is when He does things, the devil brings his facts to turn them to his side to get the credit for punishment. These are painful things that our God is going through.

When he chose King Solomon, King Solomon ended up marrying so many women and worshipping idols even though he knows they were not in line with God. Who turned him to worship idols? The whole world knows that God has chosen the Ex-president to fulfill the dream of Dr. Martin Luther King Jr. As he announced, "I had a dream that one day, it will be the turn of black people to be on the throne to show the world, we are of the same image as God does and does not discriminate." How come he ended up increasing the very things God abhors seriously? It is the work of the enemy. If you are not too powerful in the Lord, the devil will surely turn you to his side. That was why God said, "Pray unceasingly to scare the devil away." The devil is so afraid of prayers, knowing it empowers us Christians to reach out to God to intervene when is grace isn't sufficient, His power shows up. All power belongs to Him.

This is all about this book, and these are what we should fight against. And we should fight seriously and fearlessly to combat what our Maker abhors squarely, since He gave us the spirit of power and love and a sound mind with no fear. And if you allow the accuser to lure you to his side, the Father, too, will not allow things to work in your favor. Therefore, this is a war for us to fight and let whatever God dislikes to subside only by living in righteousness.

The result of this election was as equally shocking to the world as the increase of people practicing abominable sins. They are all ordered by God. If we don't think about his happiness or be obedient to his Word, he will let you know he can make us happy and can also make us sad. We saw that those whose rights were granted to perform are not equal to those who are going to suffer from the consequences. Therefore, if we just like how it happened to his chosen people for being disobedient. If we do not become an obedient nation, or be obedient to his word, we might suffer for a long time. And we should try to avoid this to reduce our suffering or else serious ones might be coming.

Now there is an assignment for me to pass it on to him to put things in order by bringing happiness back through some sort of advocate. There are also many more tragedies for all these advocators in evangelism who are being threatened to be killed by beheading and other means. This is all in the Bible from the fact that Sarah could not wait for the promised child, Isaac, and hesitantly allowed Abraham to lay with Haggai, the maid, to bring trouble to lead us into all the suffering that we are all witnessing throughout the world.

These were all prophesied in the Bible, meaning mankind is to be mindful of not having a waiting spirit to let God decide what will be best for us instead of going ahead to make hasty decisions, which always land us on rocks that are immensely going on in our lives now, being part of the fight against the evil one. This is the reality of the fact that the pot must obey the potter for its well-being and longevity. We are paying the price of the impatience of Sarah, and we don't have a clue on what to do with these groups against the whole world to the end.

The background picture is that Muhammad, out of the descendants of Ishmael, came from God in a different fashion and used force to fight people to follow God through forced obedience. Jesus came out of the promised child, Isaac, who came to show us the way to his Father and shared his blood on the cross to make a covenant of grace for our sins to be forgiven. The differences of the two were that Muhammad died and could not rise, though not rotten. Jesus died and rose again in three days and ascended to his Father back for his crown.

The Muslims do not play with their kind of worshipping God and seriously follow the rules. They do not understand the lifestyles we carry if we are the descendants of the promised child and have been liberated by Jesus, which they could not benefit. Our behavior and lifestyle seem peculiar to them, forgetting that Muhammad was a human being like me and you. And Jesus was the Son and the Word from the beginning with God. Jesus came in the form of a human being to be able to save us from the sin of the serpent and to show us the way. Isn't it strange we are still in many more sins? Satan is another strange obstructionist in the way.

Both Christians and Muslims are the children of God but have a difference in identity. And Jesus said he is the true way to the Father. His coming was purposed to give us a very important personality position through the death on the cross. The heirs to the children of the promised being, Isaac, should not be perished and should do all that seems righteous to make us the real heirs. Heirs play the role of the heir as a role and not any stigma.

This death redeemed us to become saved and formed the churches to be called Christianity to honor Jesus, who, in turn, honors God and intercedes for us. Yet majority of Christians are not taking the work we are portraying seriously to attract unbelievers to follow us to church. We advertise more than reality, and we tell people what to do but not do them ourselves.

The VIP position is bestowed on us as Christians through the grace trained in us to reject and denounce all ungodliness and worldly desires. We'd rather live upright inside and outside, devout spiritually whole lives, as an example for the present world to caution unbelievers.

Jesus is making us very important people. He wanted us to live with enthusiasm, living a life filled with beneficial deeds like being peculiar people chosen for himself, like the Israelites had been. The Christians are chosen as an example for the world that we have been redeemed from all our iniquities and that we examine ourselves regularly to live a balanced, authentic lives that the Bible is teaching us. In this regard, we can depend on God. Eating today will be enough for us, for He will take care of tomorrow. Instead, we force ourselves for all the plans that lead us into sin.

When God told the Israelites to pick the manner in the wilderness for their daily needs, they picked thinking they can keep some for the next day. The manner turned into maggots. He knows what he does for our benefit, but sometimes we do not understand him. He can't be totally understood, and that makes him God, who only does what would benefit us. He is concerned about our purpose being fulfilled than our comfort. He said, "Totally depend on me for your daily bread. Do what you can do, and leave what you can't for me."

Yet whether we're Christians or unbelievers, we are all his children if we repent like Paul, who turned to God and made a difference for good fight of faith. Whatever is your sin, if you repent, you will be saved by the grace of the covenant of the blood of Jesus. And they don't understand if they're not an advocate of Jesus. He feels like moving us from the face of the earth to stop all those abominable sins against God. They know they are on God's side. God doesn't like this, but he predicted this as part of his foundation that "they will be against every man and every man will be against them."

Father God can only protect us from them if we will stay away from the abominable sins. He had laid them for us in the Bible. Putting premium on God's interests first gets us closer to him for him to love us more, to prepare us more, and to be able to escape Satan's devices. He promised us an expected end, yet we are to do our part. The Father gives and takes, so take him seriously and not for granted because he has great love. He wants us to do things to enable him to order our steps, knowing what's best for us on our many plans.

Chapter 10

The Grieving Father

How long is mankind going to make God the Father, God the Son, and God the Holy Spirit grieve? The three of them agreed to create man like their kind. Then man was created with clay, and he breathed into him for him to become a living being just like the kind of God. And he later created Eve, specially made from Adam's rib, with curves and beauty for them to be in charge of all these beautiful things. The more He tries to love humans, the more we hurt Him with all forbidden stuff and sins.

Mankind has been making the Trinity grieve since the time in the Garden of Eden, when Adam and Eve was lured to eat the forbidden fruit by the serpent from time immemorial. Instead of being appreciative for the agreement of our creation to be the heads, we fell and were driven to suffer before we got redeemed again. Many things have gone on that we need to be more serious with life's issues and know that hell is real. Samples of it is in the system; find and watch it to help you make a decision before you are done reading this book to help us choose heaven or hell.

Lucifer, who rebelled and became the master destroyer, torments those of us created to replace him. God the Son came for our redemption, then came the burning of Sodom and Gomorrah for the abominable practices. He told Noah to build the ark, for the rain will wipe them away to start afresh with Noah's descendants. Then came the Tower of Babel made to reach heaven and see God, and their languages were divided into multi languages that they did not hear from one another to stop that project.

Noah's descendants, through Abraham to Isaac to Jacob and now to the current people on the planet Earth, has reached 6.5 to 7.5 billion. Our sinful nature is becoming chronic that we should check up to put a total stop to them and make our Father comfortable, than to make him grieving. It seems our sinful nature is crowing our righteousness. That is, a lot more people are committed to sin than those committed to try to live in righteousness and make it up to God. He still loves us regardless and tells us to come out whenever we fall to sin. Yet others are trapped to stay in it. Being the work of the enemy, we must fight hard to stay alert and stay out of his tricks.

We live now in the spiritual world to the fact that the enemy is always duplicating all original powers of God. Even though he has minimum powers, he is being wicked, making us his target. If you lose your guard and choose Satan's group like all the negativities of this world, thinking of creating your own happiness from money and wealth without even giving any consideration about Jesus and his death, resurrection, and coming to be going to church, then doing some serious, heinous sins without any remorse or renewal of the mind, you will face the consequences.

After all persuasion had failed, his loving kindness, mercy, and with judgment, very severe one without any mercy or whatsoever. Repentance, forgiveness, chastisement, and coaxing would be things of the past. His agents will come to dwell in you to commit more and more sins to earmark all kinds of wickedness, atrocities, and others for the sake of making God grieve and making Satan happy.

On the contrary, if we live according to all that the Bible teaches us along with the commandments, then the Holy Spirit will also come to live in us to help us and direct us to grow to conform to the real image of God as sinless or living in righteousness. Heaven will be for us; Jesus, God, and the Holy Spirit, a team who was pestered by the enemy, has now won the battle.

Therefore, the duties of God the Holy Spirit, as Jesus did not leave us as orphans, is to convict our sinful nature, convince, and convert us to accept Jesus as our Savior. Then we become your companion with a gentle voice, by counseling, comforting, and empowering you to the challenges of this devil and his agents. Then we read the word of God in the Bible to feed him. Food nourishes our bodies, and the word of God nourishes our spirit and soul. There is no way that mankind would be so atrocious to grieve the most important personality in his life, who made us custodians of all these beautiful creations.

The time is too far past to change our lifestyles to conform to what he wants He wants us to do to make him happy for having created us in the first place. With the whole idea of creating us and putting us on a beautiful land as stewards and custodians. We have committed so many sins already that, regardless, we could be forgiven with his love and grace, if only we could put them behind and renew our minds and focus on God, Jesus, and the Holy Spirit.

The Trinity thought of creating man like him, and he alone cares about us, so we should reciprocate his love and try to live in righteousness. When someone is mindful of you and you do not show any appreciation, he becomes fed up, then everything will escalate. Our escalation point will be going to hell. During that time, there will be no more mercy, grace, and loving kindness. We will lose all the goodness that he favored us with.

That time will be the Judgment Day. Jesus will be the judge to give verdicts whether you go to heaven or you go to hell. All signs of the latter days are very clear; Jesus is coming soon and is showing what hell looks like and what heaven looks like. Heaven is very spectacular, and hell is very dangerous and painful, burning in the perpetual fire. Thinking about the reality of hell should make us feel sad and not want to go there in any case.

Still, one cannot escape without living a righteous life. Therefore, no one should waste any more precious time in sin back and forth. The rapture, which is the same as the Judgment Day of the coming of Jesus, should start to haunt us to refrain from living for this world, which is saturated with sin. Folks, let's be serious and prepare to go to meet Jesus in heaven, or else his death on the cross will be meaningless, contributing also to his grieving.

Can we ignore our own parents and take somebody who wants to get a hold of us and end in suffering? No, we would rather stick to the one who hemmed us, nurtured us, and redeemed us through Jesus to get a hold of us again. He has forgiven our sins regardless and advises us to come back home to Him who owns us and can supply all our needs if we allow Him. Just seek him first as our Father. He knows all about us and our first love.

It means he's the one who loved us first even from the womb, yet few recognize him as our God. Until something despicable happens, then we pray for his intervention, which is painful and awful disobedience from mankind to our Maker. Praying first could have changed that situation to our favor instead of waiting till it happens and losing lives and properties. When are we going to be vigilant and not take Jesus's Second Coming for granted?

The Israelites did the same thing oftentimes from Egypt to the Promised Land. They went in and are punished, prayed and came out, and did these several times that one can balance that. How many times can we be sinful, be punished, and be remorseful and sin again and again and again, making the forty-day journey prolonged to forty years? Mere disobedience, oh! Why can't we listen to live in obedience to receive our blessings?

At the Promised Land, God himself was their king, reigning them through the prophets. Still they wanted a king, their own king. And Saul was appointed through Prophet Isaac and anointed, still disobedient, and David came. David was the best to accept his sin and humble himself before God to become his friend, then Solomon and others. Majority of them were disobedient.

Even Solomon shocked everybody with how his father, David, was the man of God's heart. He sinned and was rebuked and punished, but he remained honest to God. God chose Solomon to build his house instead of his friend, Solomon's father. He asked for wisdom and was given everything to be the most famous, wisest, and richest man of his time or even on earth or in the world and the wealthiest king in the world. But marrying many women was his downfall. He could not serve God to the end, and he almost took the throne of David. The kings Asa, Hezekiah, and a few others served him; and even in the end, some of them were not good. Among the variables, human beings are the most variable, being always in opposition to their Maker. Like how some children kill their fathers or parents for inheritance, they themselves toiled to and planned to leave them. The earlier we live right to make it to meet those who are mindful of us, the better.

He is the Potter and Creator, Jesus the Redeemer and Mediator, the Holy Spirit the Counselor and Comforter; he is here on earth with us, helping through our weaknesses till the end of time. And all the Trinity loves to treat us good and with reverence. Because He is holding us in good faith and cares so much about us, we do not have the right to choose human beings over Him.

They are immortals who agreed among themselves—the Father, the Son, and the Holy Spirit—saying, "Let us make man in our image to take dominion over all the earth, including fishes, birds in the air and all over the earth." We are the custodians and stewards for dominion who will multiply and replenish this earth and will take care of all these beautiful creations and make accounts to him. This includes our lives as well, which are not our own, and we should keep them properly guided by all that he tells us in the Bible. He will one day come for our lives when we expire; He is immortal, and we are mortals despite being created in his image.

Chapter 11

Choosing Man over God

Of late all indication of how a baby was born and spoke "Jesus is coming" and opened her arm and it was written inside. "Jesus is coming" and died at birth. Another revelation was through some pastors in dreams where a lot more people were going to hell, burning and crying bitterly in the fire. Another was through a dream by a lady from my birth country, where Jesus was hanging in the heavens and a few people were going, like ascending to him.

And majority of the women were looking on as they wore wigs. Someone's hair which some people give to god for thanksgiving. Women wearing wigs can't be a part of his kingdom, including many pastors' wives. They are not doing it deliberately, but with lack of knowledge, people will perish. Well, now we know he had revealed to us his love through dreams.

Those wearing wigs will be left behind. They have failed to ascend to join Jesus at the time in the dream, and we are to take notice for that change and be saved.

Many of these hairs for wigs are assumed to be thanksgiving offerings to gods in India. Thank Jesus for hanging up and opening his arms to receive us, and a few people could make it to him. Many hairs

that we use to sew wigs are others', and you would not know whose hair you are carrying. Searching for him as our master and finding him will direct our parts. Majority of the women could not go to Jesus—pastors' wives as well as ladies we earlier took notice to change for the better.

Get knowledge and understanding from God who freely gives, read your Bible, and ask him to reveal to us things we need to know by getting closer to him. That is why it is more crucial to serve him, know him, and do all that he tells us to do. We are only in transit and are not permanent citizens of heaven. The earlier we search for the way to join him when he gets the lives he gave us, the better for our spirit and soul. Choosing Him instead of being stubborn toward him would be the best thing to do to be on the safer side, and the Father would happily be at peace with God and ourselves.

Man was created in the image of God, but a little lower than angels, who are in charge of the errands in heaven and watch over man as assigned by God. On the contrary, man was to keep and maintain the Garden of Eden, now being the world, to keep and maintain all that is immortal. No one chooses man over him.

When the Egyptian's midwives were asked by the Pharaoh to kill all the male babies at birth, they swerved him and said that the Israelite women give birth easily. They were smart to say that they feared God than man, and in a way, they couldn't listen to the Pharaoh and obey him more than God. They refused to kill the male babies at birth until he himself took the matters in his hands and gave instructions for the boys six years and above to be killed. He got the payback and lost his son too. He has no challenger. He is supreme to all creations.

And they were punished by losing their first born, including the Pharaoh's himself. That made God exceptional, and we should seek his interests and rights first, not those of us who don't know how the world came to be and how we even got here. With that said, can a pot be more sensible than the potter? This should be the worldview of him instead of relying on our intellect and wisdom. He alone can give wisdom and understanding. Though we were created in his likeness, because of Satan's traps, we could not use his powers directly without his Son, who paid the price to purchase us. We should be very careful of what position we place him. He had shown us love, grace, mercy, and loving kindness and never passes us by, so why do we choose our right before his?

In America, our first country, and of course, the first country of the whole world, we love to give individual rights a chance and give them freedom to choose. This is something we are to think seriously about as we compare to the rights of creatures more than the Creator. You don't have to know the Bible to be able to balance this simple logic and contradict them altogether. The fact is, we should not compare the human rights with the heavenly Father's rights, which are laid down in the Bible for our guidance for those who know the Bible.

Pastors and theologians have been preaching and echoing about all the sins and abominations in the Bible for our guidelines and for our own good to protect us from His judgment. We only need to read the bible, trust, and obey to easily get all the blessings He has in store for us. The tradition of the new generation is very quick and comfortable to sin. This comprises killing, committing suicide, and unhealthy relationships involving premarital sex, which they term to be *love*.

But love is not having sex first; it's courting to know each other better, to love what she loves and cares for and know families with all background checks before commitments. In many traditions because of being not experience, naive and hasting to do things without any guidelines. Especially what God wants, the parents normally do that before the marriage is finally contracted, making them to marry for getting all the necessary blessings he has in store for us.

The tradition of the new generation is very quick and comfortable in committing sin. This is comprised of killing in many ways, committing suicide, having unhealthy relationships involving premarital sex, which they call and misconstrue as love, making them marry today and divorce tomorrow. The computer jet age means everything should be fast and naive in doing the unthinkable. They are not even getting parental blessings with marriages before leaving home with the boyfriend, then they continue with an immature type of relationship and with pregnancy, further bringing frustration if the partner doesn't turn out to be responsible. No parent can turn his or her back on their children. So protecting our children to do the right things is better than cure.

Most leave the burden on women who do not easily forsake their children. Without proper counseling, their lives become burdensome. The result is sometimes going through therapy, going through recovering because of drugs, or even ending up in prison. Satan has really got jobs to do, with the children and the grandchildren of us, the baby boomers. We have also got work to do to reverse them back to live their lives right, conforming to God, whose heritage they are, and we are going to be accountable for them before him for how we helped them turn out great to fulfill their destinies.

After reading this book, try to let your children mature with wisdom before they leave you, their parents. From my home country, they normally complete university or learn a career, start working to be equipped, and get married before they leave the parents' homes with full wisdom to be in marriages and to be in the world at large. Lacking knowledge of the wide world out there leads the up-and-coming generation to do the unthinkable, like committing suicides, having depression, and feeling uncomfortable.

Apart from what some of them who become the victims to be abused by the leaders, mentors, and even some family members were used by the enemy and continuing to use them as double victims and as third victims and fighting for their rights, which is not conducive to righteousness, but ending in hellfire with the enemy instead of going to Eternity, where the Father wanted them to be. The Son paid the heaviest price while the heavenly Father continues to find a clue as Jesus cries, seeing us still perishing because we are not paying much attention to what's going on.

A child left unpunished brings his mother and father to shame and regret. Then he will miss the good plans in store for him. Regardless of our shortcomings, God has, 100 percent of the time, good plans for his children because he brought us up for different purposes, if proper foundations are not laid down for the children to live up to them.

They missed their purpose and live immature lives to please the devil in diverse ways. The parents, being the baby boomers, will answer to God how we led his heritage. Therefore, praying for the children to be delivered from the devil's grip is our duty.

Before now in America, I heard parents were to spank their children as God directed us not to spare the rod and spoil the child. Out of frustration, some parents overdid the spanking that resulted to death. That was too bad and brought new laws to change the situation to what we are experiencing now. Still, most families keep their eye on their children to mature with guidelines and complete college and even till marriage before they leave home. It is not too late to go to the way the Creator himself wants us to go. Everything in moderation is good to help the youth know their responsibilities ahead of them for security since the fear of God as the beginning of wisdom.

All things done outside of what he wants us to do yields no good result and compels us to go our ways to tarnish his ways; choosing man's approval over God's approval is not good. Only he can lead man to be located for God's approval, as the owner of the world.

Now let's be careful not to choose man over God and to train a child on what he should do. When they grow up, they will not depart from it, to say God made a mistake to create him differently from what he was supposed to be created for. Who knows more than God?

Then do the right thing and live in righteousness to please God to receive the best plan for your child's life. Mothers usually never give up on their children easily. So it will please them for the child to turn better with a normal life than what we are talking about. Many a time, children, being part of motherhood, might not like that life; but if you could not convince him or her, you will live with it to the shame of the family. And that is planting a seed that's not properly cared for to germinate well and give a good fruit. The children are our heritage. God brings them to us to be cared for, and we are accountable to him.

God brings children to us as our inheritance to take after us. If they turn great, they make the family shine. If they turn abnormal, they disgrace the family. They do not turn great on their own accord but by the training or upbringing by the parents physically and spiritually, supported with prayers, going to church, and reading of the Bible that is full of wisdom and supported by the Holy Spirit, our Comforter. Jesus left for us that gentle voice in us who whispers to us always to do the right thing through convicting, convincing, and converting us to transform in line with Jesus and be able to be our mediator before God. They have been there for a long time and is now escalating and spreading all over here and the world. "When America, as the first nation, sneezes, the whole world coughs" which means that when we stop, the world will stop as well. Be proud to be an American and do the right things like how our ancestors started with God to build this nation.

Now He wants us to come to Him to rule his world, now these are escalating. We are so precious that he doesn't want to lose us to the opponent, who was not near during Creation and does not know how to create humans or care about us—no more than condemn us to him for judgment and be able to win us with him into the fire.

No one would like to be in this situation. With the unconditional love bond you made for them, they still suffer your own punishment for either lack of knowledge or some sort of stubbornness and disregard for his statutes. To fall victim to the enemy and opponent is very painful.

Another painful situation affecting him is how the men he chose to love the people seeing him through them with the charisma he gave them have love of the people more and to betray him. He trusted them not to choose his creation over him. They are forgiven to correct it. All are God's spoken words, just writing and adding what I know.

The one whom he had chosen to fulfill the dream of Dr. King Jr. to please the world that he created all equal and love us all equal. They both forgot where the people they love go from here by leading that kind of lifestyle to spread the shock to the world. They were both respected for how they fought for the people to make their lives better, regardless of the many obstructions they had from the opposition.

They both fought tirelessly for the people and failed to tell them the repercussions to the extent of making it a law of the land. How seriously could the clay be equal to the potter?

Since the revelation in 2014, I did all that I could to reach one of them. First by phone and later by letters to the secretary and last minute to the president to point out to them or they will lose the election if they do not make amends to this problem facing our beloved country. But to no avail. I could not reach any of them to give them the revelation, and I did not want to tell any person apart from those in the inner circle. I tried, but I failed, to my dismay. I am still trying to reach those I have been sent to for assistance to relate this whole story and revelation to them to check what they can do.

The second-chance Father, who never gives up on his children, has told me what they should do to save the people and make it up to them too. His anger is for this moment, and forgiveness and joy are for a lifetime. The Father still needs them, and I am hoping to reach them and relate the whole revelation to them, even before the book is published.

I was to meet one of them for it before they even hand it over, and I am still trying. It is my duty from him to make sure I relate all to them for action to be taken for it. When there was a gun violence, especially in schools, the way his heart breaks is equal to how sinful people end up in fire forever. And we can do something about them; there are still chances to do something for our purification. He really had true love for the people as compared.

They were going to come again if not because of this situation. They were so loved for the work where they fought for the people. Yet their ending was very painful and shocking only on this area of the world and to the heavenly Father, especially those on the side of God who could not understand how to balance the whole idea. For decades, no party has allowed it to multiply like this. And now people do feel awful embracing this lifestyle with the world ending.

As of August 25, 2017, I was watching TV and later found out how, unlike before, someone was describing how she compared being in that position from the beginning made her lost her job and now celebrating me years anniversary to encourage people to come openly,. Our Father never added this to His creation as we are his image. This is still a stigma to the family, to the society, and to the nation. Anything outside the Bible should be abolished to give God all the credits.

And now years anniversary that she announced that she was and how shock was that announcement costing her show and sponsors to do away with her. And now people are making it up to her or welcoming her openness to come and announce her true lifestyle, celebrating now with many friends and well-wishers, unlike how people were running away from her. Many wishers who came to tell their feelings at that time as well as others were also wishing her well. God loves us anyway; we should not think of hurting him.

Unlike about a decade ago, when it was a taboo or stigma, no family welcomed what God hates. Many people called to wish her a happy anniversary and how she helped them to be confirmed. The number is growing without dispute. She helped a lot to come out through her boldness. What they forget is, where do they go from here? Hell or heaven? Each decision is crucial to make a decision now.

Loving themselves and their friends, their next destination should be very important. Have they also considered what our heavenly Father is thinking? "How could they always forget my ownership and power—what I have done, am doing, and could do? Can they ignore that?" His question goes, "Even though all are entitled to their opinions and their rights, and not mine?" We should always consider God first in all we do.

That alone has proved how chances gave way to this society to grow against the wishes of the Master Planner. America, as a nation, should face the reality to revisit this situation and think about our God, if this pleases him or not. References from the Bible indicates how some cities were destroyed by fire and how some even went blind. We can't disown our children, brothers, sisters, and friends as they are part of us. Rather, we should let them know the truth to be set free. The way friends and well-wishers were celebrating with her today is a clear indication of onward growing against his will, and we have to see to it.

God wants this president to think about how he loves him, to think of the charisma he gave him to win the people, and to put His needs first before the people. And it's great to love the people and make sure the love carries them from here to heaven to make their love complete. Therefore, if we are the world, then let's start giving the knowledge of wholeness to please him. He knows we can. He is not mad at you but is waiting for you to start for him to move with you. Yes, we can. The people will move with you, for they know you love them and will do the best for them. Just change for the better, not for the worst. To please the Mighty One, we can do this. They will be grateful, and prayer for changes will be possible. Let's start now for the sake of our heavenly Father, to stop hurting Him if we love him too.

Therefore, are we going to be people pleasers or God pleasers? For the world so loved the coronation of the ex-president and all the good works and love he portrayed, I know he is among the best presidents. This part has become a dent or some indelible mark that people who love him, like myself, don't know how to conclude. I am praying for the day I will meet him to reveal what God wants him to do to come back to God for his full mark.

Please, can all the people in this country, for the sake of our Creator, feel remorse and know that it is not the idea of the people involved but the enemy who will steal their bodies and flames for his agenda of hatred and condemnation? He wants nothing good for us but just to pump us up to see that we are without any master. And you are right to do what you think is your idea or right. Maybe some relationships did not work for you, or the person you looked up to, like your mentor, has done you that to put the idea to bewitch you, as an example.

All those in this situation need deliverance, and God is preparing to deliver his children and is working behind the scenes to deliver them soon. His heart is aching, seeing all his handmade, beautiful women and handsome men embracing this abomination from the enemy and our adversary, his own creature, who rebelled against him and has been, ever since, doing all heinous things with his very children whom he created to replace him when he rebelled and was cast down on earth and made us his culprit as human being his target, tricking us.

One thing I always compare and contrast in my mind's eye is, and I quote, "God of all wisdom, power, knowing, and doing couldn't contain him up there. Then how could we?" With all respect, try your possible best, Abba Father, to save us from this predicament as you are doing. And I know he has the power to change this situation, but the earlier, the better, before his precious people in this situation die and end up in hell before help comes. It wouldn't be too late. Let's also repent as fast as we can and seek his help.

The people of God come here to intensify our prayers for those involved instead of making them feel proud to do that. The reality is, it is God's burden as the owner of this world, and it is also the burden of the people he made as custodians to make accounts to Him on the Judgment Day. We are all in trouble, especially those who gave encouragement to do and spread what God called abomination for power, which is a heinous sin or of serious evil. Yet he is ready to forgive us since He can't afford to lose us, as precious. We will be forgiven if we stop doing that.

The earlier we get to understand those who are not in the situation to pray and to receive their deliverance, the better. We don't need to waste time. He is getting ready to come for his judgment. The little and earlier we attempt his help will be on the way to assist us. If we don't do anything to help set them free, though they will go to hell, those of us who encouraged, supported, and shielded them are all going with them too to hell.

God said, "Woe unto those who know the right thing but failed to do it." Thinking you wouldn't do that, neither your son or daughter, but encouraging your friend or a relative to do that, woe betide you. And woe betide those who themselves serve as fathers or mentors who rather helped to breed this into the young ones as transference of the spirit given to them. Those who pretend to be without wives and infect those serving them with their evil intentions to turn into that kind of spirit that is now spreading in the world are also in trouble. Majority said they were serving God; using that as a cover-up, those pretenders are in trouble.

And if you are a true man of God, be alert to deliver yourself and pray to avoid such things of the devil, why they do what they have to do, however they could thwart the Father's creation from happiness. It is almost like you are a parent and are losing your son or daughter to drugs. You parents are to do anything to put him or her back on track, either by prayers through the church or by rehab—wherever you think you can get help. This is almost the same way as praying for the same God to find a way to intervene and bring those involved back to himself. His love never fails, his assistance is always in progress, and he empathizes with us in every step of the way and is ready to help.

Now our beloved president will fight for God to turn the people back to him, being mindful of where they go from here. We are all Americans who respect one another's rights as the law demands. But we are talking about the One who owns us and all mankind. His rights should be our priority and must be obeyed by the beloved people's president who becomes like Saul, who later became Paul, who didn't know he was appointed to lead us again to be corrected, reformed, and instructed to do the right thing for God. And this should be among his foundation to finish all his assignment for this presidency call to be fulfilled.

This will enable him to restore his love to a higher percentage by the world. Though few people will argue, but later, they are going to benefit more to return their love back to him as they surrender to God in a normal life, like how God created us, all his more precious creation. Including doing the right thing and putting his concerns first, he also called him to the presidency for all the world to know that the black man, too, is capable of delivering and is equally created.

We are to pay attention and adhere to what we are supposed to do to prevent our serious destruction as a nation. This could happen to us if we fail to make the changes.

As I said before, all these tornadoes, twisters, storms, and the rest are all signs of his wrath, yet as a loving Father who doesn't want to lose us, he will give us chances to refrain from sin if only we will be respectful and listen and obey. By doing so, He will let us find rest for our souls when the time comes—the time for rapture, the same as the coming of Jesus.

God will come and demand the accounts of the world that he left for us to keep as stewards. Therefore, don't let us harden our hearts and be naive to what we do, like we can challenge him. The clay can never be equal to the potter. We did not create anything to make our changes.

We live by his instructions, so let's get to work. It is the concern of the whole world to get to work. This area includes why these people feel we are sinful and don't need to live, though they are not to judge us and take the law into their hands. They think their religion is serious because they do not do that. They will be ashamed if they hear we have changed situations to even enable us also to change them from their wickedness. And our Father will help us win since we are from Isaac, the promised child.

Chapter 12

Mission Impossible

After having a series of revelations from Him and crying a lot of times for him, we are hurting him like how our children are hurting us many times when they grow up—boys become men and get married and women are not godly or caring. The parents become vulnerable as well, and we cry for our ending in the perpetual fire if the devil wins. And it's like he is winning unless something serious is done in our lifestyle changes, mainly the area of Generations X, Y, and Generation Z. The children and grandchildren of the baby boomers are talking about the American greed and think money answers all problems and amass money with all their intellect without even taking care of the poor, the sick, the hungry, the disabled, the homeless, and many more who live vulnerably. Those who use their bodies roughly, not knowing God lives inside us, is a serious sin, especially women who do prostitution, dirty or public sex for money. Beloved, Father God is living inside you in the form of the Holy Spirit. Your body is for God for having created you, of course, and not for you to disgrace him for even creating us, especially with our curves and the honey-tasting cookies that are only for marriages, leading to healthy relationships to make Him happy and proud.

Now regretting by seeing the way we think sex is love upfront sex or sex before marriage is not respectable, healthy, and not the one that Father God prescribed. He knows women are vulnerable and are the weaker ones, and the men, being cunning, will just use women to their satisfaction and dump them to break their heart just for another woman. Hence, he said to avoid premarital sex as a woman, with our vulnerability.

When a man proposes his love to you as a woman and you wait, at least, for the ninety-day rule, like what Steve Harvey confirms that God demands (courting or dating and studying each other's likes and dislikes, subject to correction of each other for at least three months, six months, or even a year for a stronger relationship before the wedding and before the honeymoon), your heavenly Father becomes the happiest and enjoys with you whatever you start to enjoy.

For the respect you have for Him to make him the third party of that marriage, then whenever there is a problem, he becomes part of the solution, making sure he covers you from the enemy's tricks. The opposite, like the upfront sex fast forward the devil inside and name all those sexes, is illegal sex. Then he becomes the third party.

Each sex before marriage brings seven demons to hang around you, and during the time you couples are supposed to be happy, then they go to our heavenly Father to ask for his permission to act roughly for having disobeyed his rules. At this time, God can't defend you, and fights escalate from day to day without understanding what is happening. Then love goes haywire and fails, leading to divorce and sometimes even ending one's life to avenge the other or others. Committing suicide is never an option as you will end up in hell and will not be free.

Around this time, you seek counseling and go back to church and to God for directions, then a pastor would declare fasting for repentance, remorse, and forgiveness within seven days, from 6:00 a.m. to 12:00 p.m. and 3:00 p.m. to 6:00 p.m., depending on any medication you are taking or on your strength.

Sometimes, you might be pregnant. But you both are to do this if you want to continue the relationship till death do you part.

Other than that, the devil and his demons will pester your lives with misunderstanding, confusion, and fighting till divorce or even killing and one ends up in prison. The enemy has messed up our lives without listening to God or going by his rules. Many are the steps of a man, but the counseling of God would only stand.

Our obedience earlier counts. Living by his commandments and statutes is better, and we should not wait till something like Hurricane Harvey in Texas happens before we pray and know our God. When we seek him earlier, the better. We can even avoid all these to remind us our sins are on the edge and that we need to renew our minds for him who owns us and has all the powers and is concerned about our purpose here than our comfort.

Getting closer to him is our best remedy. We remember that we belong to God, and we pray and ask for his intervention just like the Israelites. Waiting for some predicament before we know that we belong to the higher entity who can do everything possible makes us more stubborn. Rather, seek him before the evil days. He's the only one who knows our purpose here.

Then after displaying his powers and position to remind us of who he is to let us also know whom were, he again has feelings for us and later redeems, restores, and helps us with comfort and support from others to heal. There we should not lose guard and should refrain from not sticking to him. He will be forgiven and will remember no more. What a forgiving and loving Father he is. Folks, staying under his pavilion is for peace, grace, mercy, and loving kindness, which is for our lifetime, being mindful of our purpose that is coming to pass.

Mission impossible because I thought I couldn't write the book. I did not have enough words while I was writing my book, just like how Moses complains as well as Jeremiah and others. But God said, "I will give you words to write, plus the experience in this country. You can do this." And truly he is with me and is talking to me, and we are going, probably like how He was with those who wrote the Bible in the form of the Holy Spirit, who lives in us. After what I wrote in the journal about the revelations, whenever I sat and typed, it was like He was telling me what to type, just like how the Holy Spirit inspired the apostles and prophets to write the Bible. He constantly whispered to me with examples, just like Moses and others he assigned. He never assigns you and leaves but makes sure the assignment comes to a complete success.

This book, which I am to write by dropping my own life story to do what the Father requires, is all about how to put premium unto his words that pertain to how to live to his satisfaction. Our Father is immortal and never dies, but he has a heart that can feel pain just like us. And this is amazing when the mortal unthinkably pushes our shoulders high and lives in serious sin. I have mentioned what some people have done in the Bible and were punished. Still, we are doing what we are forbidden to do, and whoever continues to remain sinful means they are weak in prayers, allowing the enemy to consume the body spiritually.

When the enemy uses the body to sin, that is on the condition to steal, to kill, and to destroy. After that, if you do not fight to come back to the Father by the redemption through Jesus Christ, then you are on the way to hell, the perpetual fire. The whole significance of the mission is to get you out of the plot of the enemy's grip. Being the enemy of the Father, we automatically become his culprit, and he has some powers from God, which he still is holding on to cause great mess against humanity. Our real enemy is Satan. Being his children, we have powers through the name and the blood of and the Holy Spirit's power to change the situations to favor us.

Therefore, we, being the true children of God, have the powers Jesus has brought with his blood for us. Yet until we follow the redemptive rules by accepting him as our Lord and Master, we are not covered. If we do likewise, then we are even more powerful, covered by his blood with the most powerful backing from God, leading you to heaven. This is our whole mission in this world, just passing away. The service to God and the satisfaction of the Father should be your priority on earth. Without that thinking of being smart with our feelings, it will let us go in circles, creating our own happiness till we fall into sickness, tragedy, and finally, death and ending with him losing your soul and spirit.

This nation, America, was the one that put its ship there to bring the Israelites who were suffering from the Holocaust, being put in the gas chambers. This happened when they did not listen to their God, whom they know from the time of Moses through the exodus to the Promised Land. They were the chosen people among all the people on earth. Still, all that they were asked not to do, like worshipping man-made idols, they still did. Or not to intermarry the people on the land he has given them; they still married.

The great book talks about all that they did to God over and over against all the goodness, mercies, and miracles. Likewise, in our great nation, those obedient to him are less than those who do their own thing. With this, serious calamities would be coming upon us. It has already started. He can allow things to happen and can stop calamities from happening. The all-powerful God. Don't be naive, but cherish and fear him for all he can do and has done.

He did so throughout their forty years in the wilderness. Reaching the Promised Land, they still made ungrateful things against the God of their fathers, the God who they have known who rescued them and defeated their enemies, and the God who gave them their land. These resulted in all those sufferings of being captives and ending up in gas chambers. And Americans are aware because the Bible said them all, and we went to their last rescue. Can't we learn something from it as of now? Greed and money, disobedience, running away from facts, and evil, like Satan, are winning. Oh, my God, help us. You alone can do wonderful things.

Serious sins are on the rise in our country! I am afraid of the same wrath coming to affect us even though he loves and forgives. The displays of Mother Nature are the signs of his wrath that we are to take notice, because the occurrences of Mother Nature are too rampant here as compared to other nations. They don't happen as often as they happen here compared to other places—more often and many deaths. Supposing the storms and hurricanes are fire, what are we going to do? That will be a miniature of hellfire.

His punishment that allows tragedies to happen to his people, the Israelites, and all of us does not mean he is done loving us. It is to keep the rod and not to spoil the child. God chastises those he loves to renew our minds for the better. His people, the Israelites, went to exile or into captivity and returned home many times according to the Bible. Yet they were his chosen generation to show them as an example to the whole world of the way he loves the people. Despite that, they refused to totally obey him and to avoid various punishments made for them to renew their minds to pray and come back to their God many times for deliverance.

All indications of dreams and revelations are saying that God is coming soon when the rapture enfolds. Many people have dreamed that Jesus was telling them to tell others to stop committing crimes and sins and was showing the nails through the arms and the rib, saying, "See and tell others." On one occasion, someone dreamed that he was hanging in the air and that the people were ascending to him, but only a few people were able to join him in the air as I wrote before.

We should let this time of the Hurricane Harvey be an eye-opener for us to refrain from all heinous sins to cool the Father's heart and increase his love. He loves us regardless; he wants all of us to become sinless. Though not all of us can do that, if many of us start doing and praying for those who cannot stop, then they too, can be delivered through our prayers by the Holy Spirit, who will convict them to make them feel bad and become remorseful to change and need conversion into eternal lives. Nothing is impossible to God, prayers can move Him.

All Christians' intercession in the filled churches will give deliverance for our lost brothers, sisters, and children who have been so affected or naive, not knowing what they did wrong. The churches should set up intercessors to pray after evening services and pray to God to forgive our sins in all the states. Instead of self-interest, it should be God's interest first—as simple as that. Our repentance to live righteously will stop all these Mother Nature disasters. Though we were created in His image, there are so many great things he alone can do and stop. These hurricanes, storms, and others can be stopped if we listen, trust, and obey him.

The stubborn and stiff-necked people He created include the Israelites, the Americans, and the world. Instead of His original plan of creating people for his pleasure and leisure and for him to commune with, his own stubborn son, Lucifer, has changed the plan. And we are His and not for Satan. He had to do every possible thing to redeem us and not lose us the purchase price that had been paid by Jesus over two thousand years ago. Hence, all these warnings and punishments to put us back on track and meet his needs or to conform to his statutes do not seem to be working. That is why we need a change to come our way soon.

Therefore, all fearful and wonderful things are going on, even to take lives to make him the bad guy. We are the stubborn children. How the parents rebuke and punish their children when they do something wrong and later pamper them to come home and even eat is the same. Even though our parents love us and never lose track of us, God's love is much more. It is unconditional and forever to eternity. Just think about His only Son—He gave him away for our sake not to condemn the world but to compliment what was at stake, law and grace.

The painful aspect of the whole situation is that the opponent can't create a human being, but with what God has created, he comes to steal the body and lets his evil spirit live inside to cause sin. And he later leaves you to face the consequences that is his hell. When you ask those who commits crimes, they don't even know what happened to them, especially once the killing spirits has left the criminal. He is weak in prayers and had gone to another spiritually weak person. Then they regret and ask what happened or what went wrong and later become confused, he operates like that.

How do you become spiritually weak? You have not accepted Jesus Christ as your Lord and Savior. You don't go to church, and you don't read your Bible, or you went to church from your infancy and not anymore. You can't live here in transit without knowing why you are here in the first place. In the olden days, especially during the time of any king who does not have respect for God Almighty and leads the people to worship idols like the god Baal, sun, moon, and stars, he would pronounce his upcoming punishment like allowing the Babylonian king Nebuchadnezzar to besiege Jerusalem and Judah took them captive, defeated through wars, famines, and other various punishments to learn their lessons.

He does these through the prophets, especially the prophets Elijah, Isaiah, Jeremiah, and others. And when they were told and started fasting and said prayers, He heard and forgave, saying, "If my people would call Me upon Me and be submissive and humble themselves before me, I will hear them and heal their land. Healing their lands from wars, Mother Nature's disasters, or anything pestilence and disastrous to claim lives like it did in the Bible."

Now there are wars elsewhere. Mother Nature manifests in United States many times, and we keep on rebuilding. He said also that when we see these things, it means the end is almost here. That is even more reason why we should be careful of how we live and manage our lives compared to His likes and dislikes, and not to be conformed to what of this world, and to be transformed His nature.

Though it is courageous, always rebuilding and standing with one another, as our nature, how about our reverence and respect to him as our First Love to stop them all from happening? He looks through America to see the world. Though Israel is his heart, America is his eye.

Let's get smarter as being smart already, finding a lasting solution to all these as well as to any war emerging from anywhere. This is awful. Hurricanes Jose and Katia, too, are getting ready to follow. They were not so rampant during our ancestors' era. Sins are on the increase.

No more losing our citizens, nor our men and women in uniform. We have lost many already for other nations. Now just some respect, and we can live in harmony with God as our God, who even allowed us to call him Abba Father. Let's stop grieving him for having even created us into this beautiful world in the first place for his first love.

America now, as I said, is like the olden-day Israel. Either they become captives to other surrounding nations or face wars to be defeated. They get victory when they stay away from sin. David was a man of God's heart and usually didn't lose any battle. When he sinned one time and got reprimanded, he repented and was punished. That was it.

He was afraid of God and made him the First in his life and all the things he did. So God loved him and gave him peace. Let's follow his example and be at peace with ourselves. David was the best king of the Israelites, Hezekiah, and a few others. Let's live loving Jesus, following his examples, and live like we are really his image to glorify Him. The main thing is that he loves us to live almost like Him as his children.

America is not at peace at all now, with Russia's investigation and the election and North Korea talking about war. Though we are the superpower on wars, still we are to pray for His grace and empowerment just like Israel. We have lost people and money in Afghanistan and Iraq, but we were never declared a winner and kept on spending and losing soldiers.

Hurricane Harvey is not totally the end, and Hurricane Irma is also emerging in the island of Puerto Rico and in Florida. The complete wrath of God is on the move as signs of end times, and what are we supposed to do now? Let's all be alert and stop committing more sin.

Many satisfactions to the flesh are sin. Live to satisfy the spirit for forgiveness, for peace of mind, and for choosing to live for the Spirit.

There is no need for repairing and grieving if there is a way to be his people, and making him our God can stop many disasters from occurring. He said to accept that he is all-powerful and all-knowing everywhere, at the same time, without any comparison. Be amazed with Him and what he does since the whole world belongs to him. He wants me to explain things, and he leads me to contact or locate those he wants to do the assignments to work with them and to enable Him get his children instead of losing them to the opponent.

I employ others who are free from this sort of abomination to be serious and pray with Christians, His beloved people, for all those who have fallen victim to the enemy to offend God. "I have taken my time and energy to create while he does nothing but destroying them, leading Me to fight for the right things to be done. I need my people.

"Since my own son, Lucifer, the morning star, rebelled against Me and my kingdom by trying to take my throne to lift himself like Me and failed, I have been fighting and finding any means to get my people. The coming assignment is one of a kind, and this individual was created for such a time like this to be sent for this special case. The faults need corrections to enable this assignment to become possibly complete."

Our prayers as partners on earth to move him to work will be very appreciated to move his miracles to deliverance for those involved, and he will reward us with blessings. Else, he is more rebellious because he will soon be put in the fury pit with his winning people and those agents who worked for him. No time to be wasted by putting us into more serious trouble.

Now adultery is allowed in South Africa. Men or women can no longer repudiate others for adultery. The United States confirmed that all countries in the world are to build good relations with the great power and practice. So is there any power greater than that of God?

Homosexual marriage (woman and woman or man and man) is comfortably declared and no more a taboo to the families and society.

One country had just signed the law to declare that there is no more incest that a brother and his sister can marry, that a father can marry his daughter, and that a mother can marry her son. Were these written in the good book, and what chapters? Are we by ourselves and merits?

Another city is now proclaimed as a city of public sex. This means that on the roadside, church, market, football field, and everywhere you need sex, you can do it. Wow! Is this how our ancestors taught us? All are shameful and disobedient to God. These were not how our ancestors taught us, brought us favor, and blessed us. Why now?

One country allows bestiality (sex with animals). In another country, pornographic films are allowed in high schools and universities. On the authorization of the prostitution of minors, Marg Luker declares that any young girl from age ten can feel sexual pleasure, and no one should defend that person from discovering how her body feels. But our forefathers taught us of puberty at the age of eighteen years and even twenty-one years. Let's grow to please him.

Oh, my God and my King, many hearts are broken and are aching from how you are seeing people you love doing what you have forbidden them, for being so ungrateful of how you are mindful of us and created us into this beautiful world and all that it contains, where you made us custodians, and yet you are being rewarded with these heinous sins you abhor so much.

You made the world like a journey for us, that we are passing to the next world called heaven, knowing us before an accident with our individual unique purposes written near our names in the book of life.

Keep an eye on us so we can fulfill our purposes for accountability as your custodians living in all these beautiful things, being aware that we did not create these ourselves; neither our being here is on our own accord.

Are we even aware that we were made by God and for God with our purposes to be fulfilled on his behalf? Even before your conception for incubation in our mother's womb, regardless of your parent's situation, you are not an accident—by color, ethnic group, or the country you are from.

Men learned computer from his wisdom, and he had computerized everything about us individually. He taught us how to live in godliness for the proper keys to be clicked for purposes of accomplishment. Yet now majority are claiming unfulfilled lives, commanding premature deaths. Committing suicide is nothing to us since we have been taken captive by our adversary, mainly the youth who are naive to his tricks, only living by the rules of the jet age without any knowledge of God.

Chapter 13

The Changes We Need

God, with all his might, had to fight for the people he loves. God saw that, and the people witnessed it too. During his inauguration, people cried. We cried because we never thought that day will ever come. The day to answer that dream of Martin Luther King Jr., at long last, came to pass. Unbelievably, it became a reality—a black man as an American president.

Telling us how great our God acts and how great is his faithfulness. He is no respecter of persons; he had created all as equal, with color not a barrier at all. We are all important as his image in his eyes and will not, in any way, be discriminated.

The fight and love of the people that he fought with all his might and body and that we all witnessed entailed many obstructions, that if any president have gone through in the American history, probably because he was black. His love and bravery out of frustration carried him to go the extra mile to do that to more chances he gave for their increase than any other president who knew they were an abomination to our Father. Even if the law favors them, they are not right before him.

That made him hurt his heavenly Father, who called him in the first place to confirm the inclusion of blacks in the American history, dreamed by Dr. Martin Luther King Jr. I know he equally loves God and might not do things deliberately to hurt him, but due to the situation that he found himself at the time, he was compelled to take an action not conducive to the world and to God. His highest coronation proved his acceptance.

Despite all they have gone through, the dream that Dr. Martin Luther King Jr. had before he was shot had been confirmed by the Almighty God. If they fought the American wars, then they could be in the White House seat too, to honor God, who regards all the colors he created.

It was like when he called Solomon as the wisest man on earth, plus riches. He ended up marrying many women and worshipping their man-made gods, which are also abominations to him. Reversing them will be great.

Saul was chosen as a king of Israel and was being instructed by God through Prophet Isaac, whom God sent to anoint him as king in the first place. He later did a sacrifice without waiting for Isaac's instructions from God and did his own thing. The answer he received was that obedience is better than sacrifice. We, too, must obey the Father 100 percent of the time as our first love and our first in all manners pertaining to our lives.

For the president to allow his love plus that of his vice to choose people over what God wants has let them lose the seat because they lost the Evangelicals, the lovers of God, and his statutes. Though they might be Liberals, many predecessors never gave that chance. And they are also aching now, though he did not support that group and refused abortion, which was good. Yet what is going on needs answers.

Every sin is a sin before God. He had not bound that group, coupled with the indictment in the elections. What is our fate now? Men seem to be more power packed than the Owner of the power himself who

chooses them. He has all the powers and all the answers. He deals with those who mishandle the powers pertaining to abusing his people.

He wants them to effect the changes, which is still shocking to the world, especially to the Christians and Evangelicals as to what God wants. This will let them be loved completely to his changes of their governance and for God to fully know he answered the call God assigned to them both, which goes with them to advocate by themselves or through their foundation. Just how to tell the world that they love the Father and his rules and statutes than the people, concerned with the growth of the gay society against the Father's wish.

The world against the wishes of the Master Planner. America, as a nation, should face reality to revisit this situation and think about our God if this pleases him or not. With references from the Bible, it indicates how some cities were destroyed by the same issues and got burned by fire (Genesis 19:4–29) and how some even went blind. We can't disown our children, brothers, sisters, and friends as they are part of us. Rather, we should let them know the truth to be set free. Probably they have not read the Bible. Rather than celebrating and well-wishing them of their courageousness to come out. The present day is a clear indication of onward growth against his will, and we all know that. What we refuse to accept is how the hellfire is also awaiting for those who sin, and that is the number one sin.

Think about how He loves you, the charisma he gave to you to win the people, and how he has to put his needs first before the people. It's great to love the people and make sure the love carries them from here to heaven, making your love complete. Therefore, if we are the world, then let's start giving the knowledge of wholeness to please Him. He knows you can. He is not mad at you, but He is waiting for you to start for him to move with you.

As another part of "Yes, we can," the people will move with you, for they know you love them and will do the best for them, and they will listen to you. Just change for the best of the best, not the worst of the worst. Pleasing the Mighty One will be able to tell what you did with the life given to you. That will be the Judgment Day, and there are only two things to convince God with.

1. Do you accept my son, Jesus Christ, as your Lord and Savior and as the only true way to me, God? That will be to check your spiritual background.

2. What did you do with your life? Your gifts being your talents, love, relationship, and all the resources that I, God, gave to you to fulfill your purpose.

Allow these two questions to prepare you on how you live your life without any doubt. Only love your neighbor like I had loved and lived in righteousness and follow what the Bible is saying from my inspired spoken words.

Others like to fight for rights and equality to make it the law of the land during the time of our beloved brothers, daughters, and sons, thinking they deserve that. And what feeling do we have for the one who gives and takes lives? The owner of the clay who turns them to kinds of pots? Those who listen, respect, and treat their parents with respect, honor, and love have more blessings and fulfilled lifestyles with dignity, can make a difference for their generation, and will die peacefully to meet the heavenly welcome by God Almighty.

On the contrary, those who put the power into their hands and forget how they got here to create their own happiness are manipulated by the opponent to live for the flesh and die for the flesh, to put the flesh in the perpetual fire forever. He respected us as his image and gave us choices to make. If you don't become mindful of the higher entity, then you are on your own, doomed like what happened in Sodom and Gomorrah's judgment.

History reminds us in the Bible of what happened to those who practiced such lifestyles. What makes us bold, knowing that could happen to us too? Being the survival of the fittest to fight our own battles, leaving him out. He knows that deception of the enemy will be part of us. Bring this assignment to step into deliverance. Those who have ears to listen, let them listen; those who feel right to do their own thing, we will give them individual accounts of our lives on earth. Those who passed away being in love of this lifestyle will come back in dreams to tell us what they experienced to enable others to make changes earlier than nothing.

Those who are not among them but fight for them to do that are also going to face equal judgment. If you don't feel like doing that, why do you shield others who may be naive or innocent to do that? You are equally guilty. Beloved, beautiful, and handsome people of God, think and think again. The Father is waiting for the prayers of those who care to deliver them to himself. The fact that your relationship with the opposite sex did not work does not mean no lover is out there for you. The same sex couldn't produce babies, and this is not of God. Thinking of adoption, if God created that, who will give birth for people who adopt? Our population would have decreased by now.

There is one waiting for you. Steve Harvey is very good in the connections of lovers, so are Christian Mingle, eHarmony, and others. The reasons why relationships do not sustain is mainly because of how we rush into relationships. The Creator took Eve from the rib of Adam, and Adam said, "This is a bone from my bone, a flesh from my flesh," and named her as a woman, meaning "out of a man."

Just give yourself a year or two and pray for that man whose rib you were taken from to come with the help of God to be your better half. This is your prayer: "God, I pray to you to bring that woman you took from my rib to come and be my better half."

Beloved, if you pray this prayer prior to getting into a relationship, it should be healthy, and it will please him to bring you the right one for a blessed marriage to honor him. That relationship will be for the "better or worse, till death do you part." And relationships that start without prayers but only sex breed divorce. It is unhealthy, allowing the devil's interference. Early sex before marriage honors Satan. That's why when you settle to enjoy, he brings many confusions for divorces, because he never wanted our happiness. Preserving your marriages means obeying the Father's golden rules on healthy relationships on marriages.

He deems it very honorable and is always the third party in the marriage to help us trash the evil one whose agenda is forever thwarting our happiness with disobedience to God.

Out of frustration and loneliness, the enemy puts in your mind that your equal partner will not give you troubles; therefore, you look for one. He did it to that mentor, father, uncle, and priest who did this to you for the very first time, making you think it's normal, and it has reached your turn. Other agents are in the form of witches, wizards, demons, territorial spirits, spiritual wickedness in high places, fallen angels under the sea, and principalities who never sleep until they make one a victim of destruction. Their only mission is to pump you and let you sin to destruction for the heavenly Father to lose you. Hear this and be alert instead of losing your guard. Stand on your grounds, love God, and save your soul for eternity. His best interest is us. Our benefits are his joy to celebrate on your purpose. Failures are his pains.

The fact that the changes are crucial goes like God loves his people. Look at the things on earth that he had created for us to manage and be mindful of him till we meet him in heaven to make our accounts. On the contrary, the people's president also loves his people and fought with all he had on leadership benefits for the people to live comfortably on earth and not in heaven. That's why our heavenly Father, knowing the heart, allowed him to call him for that leadership and wanted him to make amends to allow the people he fought for to benefit both on earth and in heaven through the biblical lifestyle and not the earth cravings that will pass by. And his ways are eternal to meet us in heaven for the peace unending.

This will be equal to that of him who created us and loves us and to also answer his call as the faithful leader deputizing for the Master and to give answers to the world who celebrated his coronation but kept quiet to his ending, pertaining one mistake contributing to their loss. Since only God can confirm a leader, all things happen for the benefit of those who love God. Every good and perfect gift comes from him. He knows all the answers to all. Knowing him ahead makes him cover your back against any evil intentions of the enemy.

In conformity to this, his foundation should portray righteous living to teach the people he loves how to live to please the higher entity so as not to miss heaven, not to live according to your thoughts, assumptions, and choices in this world instigated by the enemy, who is only waiting for your suffering. Your choices in the world by the flesh is satisfaction to the enemy, the devil. Your choices in the spirit of humility guided by the Bible is satisfaction to the Holy Spirit, who lives in us. For Jesus who purchased us so expensively with the most precious blood, which is not supposed to go to waste, accepted us for how we are. Therefore, he wants you no matter how much you sin. He is aware and ready to clean and sanctify you till you are purified. We are for him, and he has all the patience to perfection.

Heavenly Father will be with him in every step of the way to talk to him and direct him in all that he should do because he is sending him as he sent Moses and Joshua. The president still has his people's welfare at heart. His charisma is still attractive; and his leadership of humility, love, and tactfulness not to lose men and women in the army is still commanding. This assignment, starting from America, would reach the whole world to complete the love for him and to complete his call. Though it will not be easy, the end will be successful. Many will embrace the agenda of Satan and his group to face punishment.

Yet further persuasion with the Bible will yield results. People who might not welcome the idea in the first place will later be involved, knowing he had fought for them before and sided with him on the same page, weighing his love before, and continuing to liberate them from some sinful lifestyle might bring good results to get closer to God. The president might have been created for the time, such as Queen Esther and Dr. Martin Luther King Jr., who also fought with his blood for him to bring the answer to complete this story on the dream he had. He said he might not be alive but will come to pass. That dream has come now.

When the time comes, let us, beloved people, support and pray for his success not for anybody but for Jesus, who sacrificed his blood and is still crying and interceding for us to continue shielding him to complete this assignment for his death to be more beneficial for mankind. He wants us all to benefit from his precious blood. What will be the point of his death if majority of us end up in hell? Even majority of the pastors who are driven pastors using other abomination spirits to pretend like they are working for God also end up in hell.

Being driven for quick money, they can't fast and meditate on the Word to feed the Holy Spirit in them for the supreme power of God. With that, Jesus said, "If you love me and let my Word live in you, you will do greater works, following my steps and doing more than I did."

Called. Faithful pastors are doing their part, and fake pastors start with occultism, spreading through some countries with the power under the sea from fallen angels and with demons and principalities using human parts and blood, spreading to make money and acting for Satan. They even commit us to sin and die of sickness.

What exactly do perishable human beings want in this world? We are just passing. Killing for money and wealth that you will leave behind go into the fire forever—I don't think so. How much will you eat, drink, and wear? And how many beds? Find out from Solomon, the richest man who ever lived. He assumed they are all vanity, like chasing after the wind. The only important things are to love God with all your heart, to serve him, and to do his wishes till you pass coolly to join him when the time comes, as simple as that. What's all the hustle for?

Find out from millionaires and billionaires whether they are 100 percent happy or not. It will be better for us to stop chasing money and to chase God and his righteousness; He would rather give us that inner peace, which surpasses all understanding. He said, "The peace I leave with you is not of this world but the peace from my Father in heaven, who knows what you deserve to have. This is the inner peace which reflects on the outside to the satisfaction of the spirit in you. Conforming to this world turns us against our Father. I am not rich but peaceful."

The inauguration of the people's president was the pride of all black people throughout the world and the happiness of the world's people who believe in God and accept the beautiful colors he created as equal. His finishing up saddened us with this agenda, leaving us with many questions to be answered, like the following: (1) How come the past democratic government didn't make them popular too as they were all liberals? (2) How come the past republican government never gave them the chance to grow? (3) Was the president used as a scapegoat because he was black? Many are thinking about things like these, especially the Evangelicals He was very good, but to them, God comes first and no human of any caliber is chosen over the Almighty. He was called, but why? Waiting for answers, many are baffled.

These are the questions the world wants answers of, especially the blacks, to complete their happiness and pride that a black president, too, has been on that great seat; that made many people see with their eyes in that cold weather winter morning, with tears of joy and with the greatest crowd in any inauguration. Their pride is that God created all of us human beings as equal in his eyes. It doesn't matter how some of his creatures see them. Your ethnicity and your country are now confirmed. He never makes mistakes with his chosen colors. He just laughs over such remarks since none of his creatures can surpass him, the Creator.

Many are hurting because we know it was an abominable sin to God, and with the way they know their God, they don't want to be the ones messing up his rules. They know where they came from (what they have gone through to be rich are from God), and you don't want to be ungrateful to your Master. That alone makes this assignment great to make all the necessary corrections by both leaders. The world wants to hear this to be able to balance and put things in shape and at peace for the mission to be fully accomplished. Even though they did their best for the people, they are doubting about these issues that are now growing.

There are areas to redress this issue, which is assigned to the one who is concerned to play his role; all of us people of God should show some concern too. Nobody should sit on the fence like they are not involved, nor is any family member in this situation that they should be concerned. Jesus said, "As I have loved you, love each other like that." And this love should be applied here to affect individuals in the world for the devil to lose. If he loses the world, it becomes a better place for us. And we are all to be involved for our Father to win.

After invoking you with his spirits to manipulate you to the practice, the devil again makes his followers rich to use their riches to affect other innocent, poor people as followers and win their friends. This continues to win more people to their side only in exchange for their souls, being a way of winning people to do his evil wishes to fulfill his work.

The followers should be aware that they are just trading their souls for money. The enemy's wealth is just a fake camouflage, not like that of God, who gives power to get rich like that of Abraham, Isaac, Jacob, David, Solomon, and Joseph. After passing through trials, tests, and proven stages to maturity comes wealth. In God, wealth comes with seeking his kingdom and all his righteousness, for the power to get wealth is all in the Bible.

Chapter 14

Our Lifestyle

Our lifestyle defines our attitude to condition our mind-set or mental conditioning that leads to our responses in our environment. In short, you are what you want to be, or you are what you eat. Our attitudes manifest who we think we are to control our lifestyle. That is what it means to say, "The fear of the Lord is the beginning of wisdom." Better to revere than be naive.

The charity that begins at home is built on what we go through as children and contributes greatly to our attitude, leading to questionable lifestyles we carry to show our individual habits. Most of them, too, we carry from peer pressure of friends we meet from schools. The contributions of this jet age of internet and the things we see dominating the training of the youth and young adults get from parents and schools the good and godly ones bring charity.

When growing up, especially as a boy, were you molested by the pastor you were serving, by your mentor or coach, or by your father or uncle, to give you that example as the right thing to do? Or were you going to church with your parents to attend Sunday school? The first is rather unfortunate, to fall as a victim to the devil's nurturing of the desires of the flesh, which is evil. The second is the love or charity to train you with God's principles and teachings, to depart from all sins and grow in the Lord. It is the right thing to do for his glory.

When you fall victim to the former lifestyle, the heavenly Father doesn't hold it against you, knowing you are innocent and you have become a victim, being naive. Yet gather momentum to get your willpower, and do not pursue the devil's plans. Overtake and recover your life, for the owner of your life would not leave you for the destroyer of his agenda but would rescue you for his agenda as the one and only one who created you.

He does not hold us so much responsible, but blames the enemy who possesses and manipulates the people and who, instead of being a good example, rather became an evil example to allow you to practice a poor attitude and a sinful lifestyle. He is to find a way to deliver us from this shameful predicament. We might ask ourselves, "Why should the Almighty create the enemy at all?" The answer is just like parents giving birth to children and one of them turns different that they become an embarrassment to them. Either you pray for deliverance or live with it. So try with grace and come out now, knowing it's evil.

With regard to the Almighty and Satan, the original idea was for Satan to be among God's heavenly dominion. As a handsome being and the head of the praise and worship team who appeases God, Satan allowed God to love him more to let him, the then Lucifer, the bright morning star, become a spoiled child, wanting to be like the Almighty with his powers and even wanting to sit on his seat. Lucifer's discipline turned him against his own father, and he became rebellious with some of the angels who are now his agents—the demons, principalities, and dominions behind witches and wizards. In actual life, many children do murder their mothers and fathers to take over the inheritance.

The Almighty could have destroyed Satan and his fallen angels. Maybe he left them to exist for the purpose of pushing mankind to also constantly serve and pray to God and make him the master of our lives.

Look at Job's story in the Bible; probably if things have been rosy and on the silver platter for us all the time, nobody would bother to pray and seek God's help.

Even in real life, if someone looks for a job and prays to God and gets one, he is now going to work, and praying becomes not crucial anymore. Just like the rich people, how many of them pray? The heavenly Father might have let Satan stay for a purpose, and when his time comes, he will put him in the fiery furnace perpetually to endure with the people he had won to his side in sin and abomination. Their souls are held captive with him to sin continuously for their punishment.

Sins, knowingly and unknowingly committed, are all sins that demand judgment. Abominations are heinous sins that God had totally forbidden us, like what Moses did experience through the Israelites who sinned, some openly and some behind closed doors. He lifted Ezekiel to show them how some hypocrite elders are worshipping man-made idols and images and the stars and sun that God had created. When they were punished with wars, exiles, famine, pestilence, and other disasters, they prayed and fasted for redemption. Still they did them, which are on the increase, giving the devil the chance to load us with tragedies.

Typical ones are using mentally ill people to kill our children in schools, which happens here more than in any other country. The more we sin without remorse and repentance, the lesser God can protect us in our stubbornness. While children and innocent people are dying, more lobbyists are refusing to amend gun violence laws for their gains. Why? Because it can never happen to them. The train crash from Washington could be a wake-up call to renew our minds for our interests by doing what God wants for his people.

Americans, unlike the Israelites, don't even pray seriously to stop Mother Nature, to stop disasters. Recently, in September 2017, the Philippines prayed in the name of Jesus to stop a storm from happening. You could see the sky was very dark as it was getting ready to move.

They started praying for about an hour, then the sky turned clear to white. Very amazing. For His love, he will do everything for us if only we will obey.

All things work together for good to those who know God. We can also pray to stop things from happening. The Father is no respecter of persons and loves us all regardless. That was why he had patience for the Israelites who messed up several times, and he chose the Americans to deliver them from the Holocaust as his people. Then we have to deliver ourselves with prayers and fasting and reading our Bibles to know the real truth and be free.

In our situation, he is going to send the people's president, like how he sent Jeremiah or Ezekiel to do the job of restoring his people back to himself. He has all the plans, knowing all things from the beginning to the ending. Only the president will have to agree and pursue with our support for being part of the agenda. Other than that, what we call Mother Nature is full of his wrath to tell us to stop our sins, which leads to destruction. Starting it will be a crusade for many to follow. With knowledge of awareness, his love will be increased to cool.

Do we like to stop their occurrences than always building? Yes! Death and loss of properties involve starting all over again and again and is always more painful. Obedience is better than sacrifice to protect our lives and properties. The Bible said, "Trusting and obeying yield good report to subside the Father's end-time wrath." Witnessing them doesn't make him happy. Yet we have become like "spare not the rod to spoil a child." We fail to listen.

Taking notice and refraining from evil lifestyles lead him to regret having even created us in the first place. It is painful to be in such a situation many times, and he has been witnessing them as we are his people and is aware of everything going on with us.

When Father God sent the prophets on his assignments, there were a series of distractions. Despite his directions, though he displayed his powers and punishment and some died, those left humbled their hearts to become his people as he also becomes their God.

By listening and obeying his directions, he will have pity on us, redeem us, and make us the people just like those whom Jesus saved. The changes will be eminent. My prayer is that he doesn't come now as I have also delayed by not reaching those involved. Due to that, he doesn't come now as I have delayed in trying to reach those involved to help and getting distractions.

The changes will be in the personality of a man who is good at speeches and on what it takes to make the changes that the American people will love, especially the baby boomers. Many youths will embrace it. The Evangelicals, Christians, and many in the world will love to follow and work hard to please our heavenly Father. After all, everybody loves to go to heaven instead of hell. Hello, America! Let's fight to strive and make those in it feel the stigma to stop like before. The Bible declares in Leviticus 18:22–30 the most abominable sins. Lots of them are declared unhealthy by him to those who are practicing publicly all that he hates.

Recently, I heard it was declared in Australia that 63 percent are in favor of this kind of marriage; Britain accepted it also. A lot has been going on in the US. In New Jersey last week, two women pastors got married, which is very astonishing. A woman from one country brought her male child, who went to one of the elite schools, to a male in another country to marry and to have sex into human excreta in his anus. Wow! To put the most expensive blood, which can produce a human being, into the dirtiest human product that is to be dispose-off, what kind of mother is she? God is so saddened and is asking himself, "Is this the world I created for my people for my glory?"

The elite countries decolonized, especially other countries, with the concept of marriage of one man to one woman against polygamous marriages of one man and many women. As if that was not enough, there's a man to a man and a woman to a woman. So what happens to multiplying and replenishing the earth? I mean, to multiply and fill the earth, as what God said.

What does this woman want? Does she value her own son, or did she do that to find cheap money, instead of a normal marriage, to give her grandchildren? Only few women can do this strange, devilish thing. Really, this world is being manipulated by the evil entity and their powers, making us unimportant. Does their boss, Satan, put into account all the importance of the science of chromosome, anatomy, and physiology, of the formation God put in place, to use our bodies like this? The son's mates were astounded and could not balance the situation, knowing the guy was brilliant at that elite school in his home country.

Do people read the Bible at all and accept the words dictated by God to men through the Holy Spirit's inspiration? The world is miserable. Is the devil winning? No! I don't think so. He is the Infinite God who has answers to all things. Hence, the change is on the way coming. The genius-loving personality will come to the people's level to explain to their understanding with power-backing deliverance from the Father, the Son, and the Holy Spirit.

He knows our frame and the way Satan, from the Garden of Eden, did not leave our ancestors alone and caused them to sin to get their glory until Jesus came to defeat him.

He was and is not going to leave us alone for him, unless we don't go to him. But when we fall into sin, he does not expect us to remain down and keep on being sinful but back up and get off from it. We are to know his protection in the Word, that we are to run back to him to help us get our strength back. He is ready to forgive us; the price is paid already.

The Supreme Orchestrator, for the love of His people, always finds a way to change situations for it to work for us. He is aware of the roles of the enemy who is hunting us like a hawk hunting a chicken. Any means to incriminate us to get us accused before him are all the work he does daily with his agents. They are constantly hustling to get a soul into sin and be added to their number for judgment, which I have been stressing many times as the Father's main worry is losing us to him, the accuser.

He too, does not sleep or slumber, looking out seriously for our goodness through his grace, mercy, and loving kindness through his only Son. And he sends his Son and other prophets, so God sending him, the deserved person who is always anxious to change the situation for better, comes another change for him. And yes, he can!

In my home country, we love America, and of course, almost the whole world loves America. The world picks most things from America, if not all, as the first country. As such, when America sneezes, the whole world coughs. Most of these lifestyles are very bad, unlike what the Creator wants for us. Though he accesses what is in our heart more than our physical appearance, what we see with our eyes creates evil for others to copy blindly. This is the country where anybody can become somebody with that American Dream. Why interfere?

He is complaining more of those lifestyles that lead to sins of abomination that we all know, like sharing of blood too, raping of women, and killing them. Killing of any kind is heinous, as well as sleeping with animals, which are also capital sins. As well as the same gender and transgenders, thinking God didn't know what he was doing, wrongly creating you as such. What we should all take notice of is that God doesn't make mistakes and that nobody can do what he does with him giving you the wisdom. Can you believe that heaven is hanging over the earth? And by whose power? Can the opposing party commit us to sin to do that?

The lifestyle that he created us with could be modified by the world's development from the industrial era to the computerized era. He would not mind the difference to beautify us as we are his image, and looking at the colors of humans and birds and other things he created, we could see he loves beautiful things and creates individuals uniquely with the purpose that only you have. We should not worry ourselves to be someone else.

Satan is also making duplicates to thwart his efforts of anything he creates. He did not get stripped off his powers. He and his fallen angels under the sea, forming the group of mammy water living under the sea, plan the world's fashion for their girls to bring them here to attract us to follow suit. The girls are so beautiful and trap our men, as well as their men trapping women here, using them and sending things about them to the underworld to be able to manipulate them. Through changing bodies, having wild hair colors, wild makeup, and dressings, those under the sea are representing Satan to thwart all things that the heavenly Father is making.

In fashion, they have so many beautiful girls that when they dress and mix up with those on earth, they look so beautiful and amaze us here, and their styles are extraordinary that everybody wants some. They are picked by the designers to sew for their clients, especially the stars, movie actresses, and actors. Then others follow all over the world.

Out of ignorance, we are conformed to the world's styles, and we love them. These include hairstyles of many wild colors against his colors, shoes, and many more styles of dresses, especially for ladies. He cautioned us in the Bible, "Be ye not conform to the world. But be ye transformed to what my Spirit will be teaching you since the Holy Spirit will be living in you to direct my likes and dislikes. Though I am working on you till you are transformed as you are mine already, the enemy wouldn't allow unless you pray unceasingly. And he is constantly working behind the scenes without we in the known, and until perfection."

Majority of evils against humanity that affect the sovereign ruler are these agents by mama water family, who fell with Satan and were pushed under the sea just to plan evil against earth. In my country of origin, most are Christians that even Benny Hinn prophesied before and mentioned that my city will be producing several prophets. So many go to some of the tallest mountains, discovered by a hunter so many years back, to pray for anointing.

They go there to pray and fast to get the anointing, being the power of God all right from the Holy Spirit. Some spend years and some months and some weeks depending on the fact that you were called or were just driven. I went there to pray for healing with a pastor, not believing I had a call, though I had been told and was confirmed there too. Especially the young among them, when they got the power and they come to open their churches, growing and booming with prophecies, then these people under the sea will send their girls with sparkling beauty to join the churches to entice the pastors to sleep with them and to fall.

You know men and beautiful women. Then they got the Holy Spirit's power from that wonderful high mountain they prayed for, and when they sin, the Holy Spirit will depart and the familiar spirit from the devil will replace it. Still they can be used to prophesy. God did not strip the powers of the devil when he knocked him to the earth. Now they become the candidate of the enemy instead of God. They don't discern to find out or be delivered by a senior prophet. They continue to live in sin, and their souls become the property of the devil, sometimes unknowingly, until delivered or killed by the agents of occultism if they seek other powers for their churches and pretend to be using the anointing of the Holy Spirit.

Others also follow friends, and some senior pastors who have already gotten their powers from under the sea perform some horrible rituals to get them quick money in exchange for their souls—meaning you're accompanying him to hell. In this case, the congregations will be lost to Satan for hellfire too. This guy and his co-host are not resting or sleeping. They are only planning evil evidence to incriminate us into hell with him. It is his only agenda.

In marriages, the sovereign ruler said, "Court the woman and study her if she is the bone of your bone for about at least six months to a year, even months before you marry and go on a honeymoon for Me, God to be with you and enjoy with you and let you love each other as a third party till death do you part as you obey the vow." On the contrary, the enemies' rules are totally opposite. We start love with sex, and as with our enemy, sex is never love but a devil's trap.

Sleeping with another woman immediately allows the devil to cause many troubles of fighting, divorces, and even killing. Then stress leads you to mate with the same sex for your happiness, which causes abomination, like Sodom and Gomorrah, and God will punish you of any kind because he really hates that. In all areas of our lives, the devil is playing evil negative to hinder his grace, honor, loving kindness, and all that Jesus won for us. This guy is playing it hard by hook or by crook for us to lose our potential predestination before we get there.

Nevertheless, he allows us no chance to enjoy our custodianship, the honor God accorded to us to take charge of all he has created and to give him an account. Generally, the lifestyles that many are portraying are formed by the devil under the sea. The wigs are dominating our natural hairs, and their wild colors, among other things, are all styles from the sea.

In my country of origin, a very beautiful, peculiar woman came to braid her hair, and the master ordered the girls to complete it quickly. After three hours that they were supposed to complete braiding, they still have not done half. When they started complaining, they are all together, but the woman vanished to go under the sea. One of them who complained said Jesus and was found on the beach, while the other two ended under the sea with the woman as they came back to tell their story. Under the sea is a nation by itself, and people go there for various powers only to sin. There is a sin city under the sea.

Apart from their control of styles or fashion, they are also involved in our individual lifestyles by trying to turn the good destiny that God has created for us to portray and to benefit us to live for him upside down to live for Satan. He will fight you with tooth and nail to turn your destiny to the negative way and confuse you with his negative lifestyles of sin and abominations to accuse you before God, thus getting a full chance into your life and mess up with you. He would like you to be a prostitute, a drunkard, a rapist, a killer, or an abuser and give you any vice to distract you with to take you from your destiny of glorifying the Creator.

We are at war with our brother, the accuser, every now and then. Our Father wants us to seek him earlier and find him to protect us twenty-four seven. The devil and his agent cause war and tragedies if they want human blood for their rituals. They just manipulate a human being to kill, like what happened last night during a concert in Las Vegas. This sixty-four-year-old retired accountant was shooting from his hotel room, killing about fifty-eight on October 1, 2017. The devil was manipulating his personality. If he were alive, he wouldn't know what happened.

The change is eminent and is coming with the man chosen by the Father, like how Jesus was chosen to advocate those lifestyles and attitudes, being transformed to what he wants to live for him to glorify his name, allowing us to fulfill our destinies and meet him in heaven to enjoy our mansions in paradise with the Sovereign ruler. Be prepared for this revival. Then change for the best has finally come. To make sure we choose God first in all our encounters and deliberations, His mark of protection from the enemy is on us.

Put God first in all things we do since man did not create himself, nor did we get here by accident. The Supreme Orchestrator carefully orchestrated things to happen the way we see and gave us wisdom to add up what we are supposed to add up. Who do we compare with him? How can a perishable human being's interest be recognized first before the interest of the Immortal? As far as we surrender to Him, he knows the best for us as we rely on him.

Upon that, we can't be men pleasers. The Hebrew midwives were instructed to kill the male babies of the Hebrews by the Egyptian king pharaoh. They knew God first and did not please the king, which could have caused them their lives. God did not let it happen (Exodus 1:15–17). The same way Shadrach, Meshach, and Abednego did not bow down to the golden calf of the Babylonian king Nebuchadnezzar, and were put into the hot furnace seven times yet never got burned because God sent an angel to be with them and cooled the fire. Even the soldier who threw them in got burnt and died.

So as Daniel who refused to bow down to the king's golden calf, whenever the trumpet sounds as the people of Israel they know they always choose God first or face the consequences ended them to serve the king of Babylon since they know Him and all the miraculous things and punishment he can give, but his love is eternal and must be obeyed. Our righteousness and obedience make us be at peace with our heavenly Father.

Chapter 15

The Righteous Living

Our forefathers were idol worshippers, adulterers, and very ungrateful to God. The forty-day journey took them forty years; that was during the exodus of coming from Egypt through the wilderness to the Promised Land flowing with milk and honey. Even though God performed so many miracles, still stubbornness was very rampant with them. Then they sinned several times. They felt remorse and fasted to humble themselves for forgiveness to overcome it and move forward, and finally, they arrived after a majority died.

Compared to today, our sins are numerous and increase past our forefathers'. After their godly foundation was built, putting God first in America, we have tried to change all that concerns God with the Spirit to our canal man of the flesh. All that God was saying were confirmed by Billy Graham's daughter when she was interviewed sometime in 2017, which I read through WhatsApp. And I am going to quote them: "A lot of people are wondering how God allows certain things to happen. And it's because we live by our choices instead of His commandments and statutes to guide us for our own good to get great results."

When Billy Graham's daughter was interviewed on *The Early Show* by Jane Clayson, Clayson asked how God could let something like the attack on September 11 happen to us. Graham's daughter gave an insightful response and said, "I believe God is deeply saddened by this, just as we are, but for years we have been telling God to get out of our schools, to get out of our government, and to get out of our lives. And being the gentleman he is, he had gently backed out. So how can we expect God to give us his blessings and his protection if we demand he leaves us alone?"

In the light of recent events—terrorist attacks, school shootings, and others—I think it started with when Madalyn Murray O'Hair was murdered. Her body was found recently. She complained that she didn't want prayers in our schools and we said okay, and some said, "You better not read the Bible in our schools." The Bible says, "Thou shall not kill, thou shall not steal, and love your neighbor as yourself," and we said okay.

Then Dr. Benjamin Spock said that we should not spank our children when they misbehave because their little personalities may be warped and we might have warped them. And we might damage their self-esteem. (Dr. Spock's son committed suicide.) We said the expert should know what he is talking about. And now we are asking ourselves, "Why do our children have no conscience? Why? They don't know right from wrong. And it doesn't bother them to kill and even kill strangers, classmates, teachers, and themselves.

Probably if we think about it long and hard enough, we can figure it out that it has a great deal to do with "we are reaping what we sow." Funny how simple it is for people to trash this wonderful, loving God and then wonder why the world is going to hell. Funny how we believe what the newspaper says but question what the Bible says. Funny how you send jokes through email and Facebook and they spread like wildfire, but when you start sending messages regarding the Lord, people think twice about sharing. Funny how lewd, crude, vulgar, and obscene articles pass freely through cyberspace, but public discussion of God is suppressed in the schools, colleges, and the workplace.

Funny how when you forward these messages, it will not be sent to many on your address list because you're not sure what they believe or what they will think of you for sending it. Funny how we can be more worried about what other people think of us than what God thinks of us. Pass it on if you think it has merit. And for readers, I deemed it a merit to be included in this book because it is the same thing that the heavenly Father is drawing our attention to, that those who trash him face judgments and punishment because sin is not part of Him. Only the enemy has been turning his children into it and against Him.

The one he created is an enemy, and if you read and it does not make sense to you, then don't complain about the bad shape that the world is in or in better shape. Either we change for a better world or we continue and all perish together in the world through wildfires, hurricanes, earthquakes, and other disasters and pestilences. Because he will punish us for our sins regardless of his love for us. Sin can never be a part of him. Though you will be forgiven, you will be chastised for the right punishment, for he wants you to refrain from it next time think twice.

For further clarification of what he related to his people, he does not share his glory with anyone, so nobody has the right to trash him or put him in second place. If anybody does anything to offend him, the one will face it squarely, like what happened to the following people from looking down upon God, the ultimate of creation and all-knowing.

The Lord God is really saddened to the extent that Jesus, near death, had revealed to many people that even with Christians who are reading the Bible, going to church, and advocating for him, about only 1 percent will go to heaven. Incredible. And some Christians agreed to the law passing same-sex marriages. And it's very serious to hear this from a pastor, as a lover of the gospel watching TBN. God, have mercy on us.

He is sad, as I quote, preaching from the Endangered Species:

> *Species Part 2.* Concerning marriages and families, saying God created us as a culture of his image with confidence, commitment, and communication with him for future peace instead of living in the world with

guessing to entail curses. He backed his preaching with the following quotations. Joshua 24:15: That Joshua and his household shall serve the Lord. Proverbs 27:17 explains if iron sharpens iron, then a man should sharpen the countenance of his friend who is worth of purpose. Also, Proverbs 3:26 and Proverb 11:4: Fellow Christians, how are we doing our jobs? Are we helping the unbelievers to be at peace with God or to be rebellious?

On April 10, 1912, the RMS *Titanic* set sail from Southampton on her maiden voyage from England to New York. At that time, she was the largest and most luxurious ship ever built. After her construction, a reporter asked the man who built it how safe the *Titanic* will be. With an ironic tone, he said, "Not even God can sink it." The result—we all know what happened to the *Titanic*. It got sunk due to the owner's utterances against God, and many lives were lost, mostly very rich people enjoying their vacation outside Britain.

And the following were quoted from WhatsApp and makes sense to be added as examples. Others took God's invitation for granted.

> *John Lennon.* Some years before his interview with an American magazine, he said, "Christianity will end, it will disappear, I do not have to argue about that, I am so certain. Jesus was okay, but his subject was too simple. Today, we are more famous than him" (1966). Lennon, after saying that the Beatles were more famous than Jesus, was shot six times and died.

> *Tancredo Neves.* During the presidential campaign in Argentina during his time, he said that if he got five hundred votes from his political party, not even God could remove him from the presidency. Sure, he got the votes, but he got sick a day before being made president, then he died.

Cazuza. During a show in Canada (Rio de Janeiro), while smoking his cigarette, he puffed out some smoke into the air and said, "God, that's for you." Not long after that, he died a nasty death.

Marilyn Monroe. She was visited by evangelist Billy Graham during a presentation of a show. The Spirit has sent him to preach to her. After hearing what the preacher has to say, she said, "I don't need your Jesus." A few weeks later, she was found dead in her apartment. Let's be careful on how we talk about our supreme entity.

Bon Scott. He is the ex-vocalist of the AC/DC. In one of his 1979 songs, he sang: "Don't stop me I am going all the way," he vowed, "the highway to hell." On the ninth of February 1980, Bon Scott was found dead in his sleep, having been choked by his own vomit.

Campinas, Spain, 2005. In Campinas, a group of drunken youths went to pick up their friends The girl's mother accompanied her to the car and was so worried about their drunkenness. She said to the daughter, holding her hand, "Go with God and may he protect you." She responded, "Only if he [God] will go with us in the boot because inside here is already filled. There is no space for him."

Hours later, they heard that they have been involved in a fatal accident and have all died. The car was damaged beyond recognition, but surprisingly, the boot was intact. The police said there was no way that the boot should have remained intact. To their surprise, inside the boot was a crate of eggs, and not even one was broken. Many, even ordinary people, have forgotten that there is no name under the sun that was given much authority like the name of Jesus.

Many have died and gone, but he died and overpowered death to rise again. No human being on earth has the right to trash God or look down on Him.

I brought this across for the benefit of those who are being naive or do not properly recognize God. After reading this book, please be an advocate yourself as you read the Bible as well to get to know him and his Word and his commandments better and to tell others to know him too.

He is too great, loving, and important to be despised. He is God, who created and who came to live with us to redeem us, and even the grave could not contain him as he rose on the third day. The same was left as the Holy Spirit who lives in all who will yield at the same time.

When the devil comes against us, God is all over us to restore, revive, renew, reward, refine, and redeem us at those critical moments to make sure we are in a normalized position and be able to live a righteous life. He is all in all. There is none like him, and no one can be compared to him. We are to love and cherish and put him number 1. The awesome three-in-one God, affectionately called the Trinity, is very mighty.

Let's face facts. To those who constantly don't bother to hurt or put our (self-interest now) sin, do we not have souls and spirits in our bodies to recognize the one who put us all together? Think about this or his formation. On our mind's eyes, do we consider the cluster of stars called Pleiades, and the constellation Orion that turns the shadow of death or deep darkness into day or night? That calls the waters of the sea and pours them out of the face of the earth? The Lord is his name. Find this in the Bible from Amos 5:8, king of kings.

Have we also considered how he hung the heavens over the earth? The land to walk on, the air to breathe that gives oxygen, the forest and the rain forests, oceans rivers and fishes, birds in the sky and their colors—have you generally considered all His beautiful creations? The seasons and times—he is an amazing God, who said there is a season for everything. A time to be born and a time to die. This kind God is full of mysteries and his loving kindness, mercy, justice, judgment, and punishment; and we must fear and respect Him more than any being we can think of. Apart from his judgment in the good book, He is still in the usual business to let you know right from wrong, reading what he did to those people you just read about. All of them experienced or paid with death.

All of them, after despising Him, had their shares as the giver of souls. How would people not fear him and not even be amazed of all that he was and is and is to come. If we live righteously, he is a real loving and caring Father around all spheres of life. The reality is that enough is enough of sins of abomination, adultery, selfishness, wealth, greed, and consciousness being committed by perishable human beings who do not take wealth to the grave.

Those who are driven pastors are those who, instead of doing pure churches that take care of the poor, widows, orphans, and the less privileged, are rather amassing wealth on the expense of the poor congregation who are hungry for Jesus to get their salvation and for security when the rapture comes. God himself said, "He who spreads the good news will be rewarded," but not to the extent of being greedy, getting multiple and very expensive cars, houses and planes, while there are poor in the church and even homeless people in the society who need help from the riches the churches as well. Please do you part to make a difference in someone's life.

We are all crying to God for our needs to be met. As Christians, we are the salt of the world and supposedly know better to help the less fortunate Christians and unbelievers to be able to draw them closer to Him, following our footsteps. The pure churches are those who are mindful of those things specified, like caring for the needy with life's encounters. Many rich people and some of the stars even do these things to be their brother's keeper.

He created us all, and all are crying to him to eat, sleep, and survive with all our needs. Upon this, he who does good to his neighbor does it for God for answering someone's prayer request. He treats it serve as a loan from you to be paid double for your trouble. There are revelations going on from God and Jesus and from some pastors and individuals that about 99 percent of Christians are going to hell during the rapture. Why? He who thinks he is standing firm should be firmer or else he falls. Thinking of being firm in the Lord might be a deception.

Because we are just churchgoers, not doing what the Bible is telling us, Jesus became poor for us to be rich; and if we get rich, we should not be complacent but share with those in need with the knowledge that we are all strangers and temporary residents here on earth, just on transit and passing by on the way to heaven or hell. We came with nothing and go with nothing; I guess we know this. Therefore, being greedy for money might be even funny.

The beloved people God created are the leaders to his projects on earth. Leaders can't turn their backs on their master with serious stubbornness, though he is aware we are bound to fall into sin. Sometimes he expects us to come out of sin without wasting time and to confess forgiveness to be forgiven and proceed with our lives. Many have overlooked this and make sin a part and parcel of us, forgetting there is any judgment waiting without escape.

And the outcomes are fatal. You will be living but hanging. You shall eat and not be satisfied and sow but not reap. Your emptiness and hunger shall remain in you. Anything you will be doing has no foundation and can fail at any time because you probably rely on your money, achievements, and intellectual accomplishments, including your wealth. It ends with you right here. The Word of God and spiritual growth will accompany you forever with the peace of God. Without spiritual covering on earth, your foundation is weak and to no avail.

The heavenly Father requires more from us after being born again by accepting Jesus as Lord and Savior, reverencing him with fear and worship, and thus begins the wisdom and skills for a good understanding in your walk with God. Being born again as a new creation allows the Holy Spirit to live in you to teach you steadily from doing the right from wrong and get you closer to him to enable him to perfect your creation, to enable you to discover your purpose, and to live in fear of sin. Our purpose, in which the enemy is preventing us to achieve, is to glorify God.

Hence, he drags us into sin constantly to stop God's glorification that our fulfillment is supposed to bring to him. The Holy Spirit assists in our conviction to stop us from being sinful, making you remorseful each time you sin and making you gradually deviate from sin and strengthen your walk with your Father through your Bible reading and acquainting yourself with his likes and dislikes. That is the road to righteousness. Then seeking him and his kingdom and righteousness becomes obvious. And all things that he knows we need—like houses and cars—and everything he knows is necessary. Just talk to him in prayers. He is very close to you and needs you to get peace that surpasses all understanding.

The reward of your righteous living that he has in store for you is great and numerous. No more running in circles. Then you show your family, friends, and neighbors the way to righteousness, the way to God. The precious blood of Jesus can pay for any sin you have committed, and he has forgiven us and wants us to come to start our righteous living to meet him in heaven. He hates sin anyway but loves the sinful and will chase you, chastise you, and make it right as the Owner of your life; and that is exactly what he is trying to do to us.

The assignment of the changes is coming to pass by the assigner to enable the assignee to assume his assignment for all to embrace and to live happily forever. He still loves us all who faulted but always works on us to perfection. The one who is to be echoed to the people will mount his crusade on the changes for righteous living. And all of you out there who will read this book too will tell family and friends to join the crusade to help and move fast with righteous living till the world comes on board with this awareness and make this world a better place for the owner and for our eternal security.

Knowing who we are, as his image and masterpiece, will help us be obedient to him and everything he wants us to do. That is why I am saying our sin does not stop him from disowning us and stop working on us to resume our position and make us perfect. He gives a second chance, which we should not take for granted. If you fail to conform to him and the devil puffs you to remain in sin till you die, then hell will be your place of abode forever, as eternity is for the righteous. The main reason why he follows us to come back to him is to avoid us ending up in hellfire. This man on earth here was made a king among his family—his wife, children, and stepchildren. He's unique table head and a leader, and the wife cares for him so much, walking in his steps to do his own thoughts, moved him away from the wife and children

Daughters on the aisles for their wedding. A king or head managed about twenty children, including in-laws and grandchildren. The family was taking care of him alone, and now they are all very rich. Suddenly, the devil pumped him up to change his gender to lose his prestigious leadership. This cost him his marriage, family, and children; and he became lonely by himself.

Even if such a thing is prompting you, why don't you have second thoughts about God, making him not know better to create you the way you were? Your children will be fatherless while you are alive. Who will walk them on the aisle when they get married? Do we think this person is happy without the family and children around like before? Now he can't turn back, and the enemy is happy to end up with him. We are to learn of his tricks and be mindful of wickedness. Now the devil is laughing with his agents accomplishing a deal.

An innocent wife got shocked for not knowing the man she married. Situations like this will take you straight to the place only God knows unless he can reverse and pray seriously for forgiveness from God and all the people whose hearts he broke. At this point, the devil has finished his work to get the soul and the spirit, who are already grieving in him. No matter how exorbitantly he is living, pretending to be happy, the soul and the spirit are grieving for the Judgment Day.

He can't say he is happy like he used to be. Self-made happiness is full of misery for your soul and spirit. Therefore, you need to pray for God's directions when such things start knocking at your door. Get salvation, and go to church to be protected from this world that we are passing through and for counseling to love who you are. Nothing is lost, yet only we were late. Still we can connect to him, having empathy with us as his mortal image.

Chapter 16

The Security of His People

He is mindful of his creation and has all the wisdom to devise many strategies to protect all his creation and will do everything to protect us and secure us with warning, chastisement, and rebuke till we yield to his commandments, just like what he did to the Israelites till they were transformed and finally rescued by the Americans, who knew the history and are supposed to do better and stop doing likewise. Probably those who knew have mostly passed away.

That even led them to be spread in the whole world that some ended up in some African countries, like my birth country in my city. He never fails in any security that he works on from the beginning to the end and prepares in the spiritual realms before it is exposed to the physical realm. The time is our turn to get the one in charge to come and follow his plan and start in motion. He will be in his palm and will whisper through the Holy Spirit all the layout plans to follow with security access to success.

No one has heard or known what God has in store for those who love him. His security is working twenty-four seven to make sure we are secure in salvation to live with faithfulness and righteousness and to enjoy what he purposely has for us—from forgiveness to success, prosperity, and the inner peace of the spirit—not the one in the world that has an end but his kind of peace that surpasses our understanding. He wants all his beloved people to be on board to enable him to sing and celebrate our success. He feels our pain and saves our tears just like what happens with his beloved people, the Israelites. He loves the world the same way. He chose them and made them an example to the whole world.

He purposely warned them through the prophets, from Isaac, Isaiah, Jeremiah, and others to Obadiah; and they failed to listen. They were punished with wars and defeats, going into captivity and going into exiles, captivities, and again bringing and gathering them on their own land and even punishing their adversaries, showing how seriously he loved them. Today, he will punish our enemies too if we forgive and leave the vengeance to him.

Though no one is perfect, and he is aware, looking at all the things he created like the land, rain forest, animals, the oceans, and rivers and fishes and human beings like his image, we have to be afraid of sin. Even the mystery of pregnancy and childbirth alone should caution us to be very careful.

For the love of his creation, he is also mindful to be protective of all of us, waiting for some of us to renew our minds and focus on him. That's why he gives rain and air to all of us. He feeds all of us; those who don't have through his angels in human form help you for him. On July 15, 2014, at 2:30 p.m. to 3:00 p.m., there was a revelation and confirmation by a prophet from my birth country that God wants to be introduced seriously into the White House due to how he loves this country and be among them in their deliberations.

I should pray for him to get a representative to introduce his agenda to the politicians to increase his security around his people. Many are our plans, but if we pray for his guidance and direction, everything works for our own good. "Everywhere my people are," he said, "I want to be among them. I am so mindful to protect and guide them from falling into so many troubles and temptations." The prophet told me to pray for someone to come from God to be among them, and I prayed and prayed and even wrote to our lady, the then secretary of state Hillary Clinton, the woman I respect so much for her fearless fight.

The letter expresses how the Father God wants us to stop those sins of abomination that has skyrocketed, and there should be some sort of awareness by the people to know about that as I added preaching to show how he was hurting and wants us to be aware and wants his beloved people to be aware of the sins of the nation to stop so many disasters.

From this year, in August 2017 alone, hurricanes have claimed many lives from Puerto Rico. In Houston, Texas, there were about 100; the shooting in Las Vegas was 58; New York, 8; Texas, again, in a small-town church, 26; and others. He doesn't want that unless the people humble themselves through the leaders to pray to stop them as they are from the devil's mechanism. Knowing God for our security is the best thing we can do and claim.

Though he brought us to this world through parental protection, he never lost track of every one of us—every step we take, every thought, plan, decision, attitude, and lifestyle, to the extent of knowing the number of hair on our heads. Our worries are his, and he likes to fight for us only good and perfect things. That is how extensive God cares.

He knows because he cares and wants us to depend solely on him to direct us to do what we can and allow him to do all the hard ones to ease the load on us. We are not to do what he is supposed to do. That makes us struggle many times. We try to his part. He also guarantees our security, allowing his part to overshadow ours to make sure we are secured in every area of our lives no matter how hard the devil will try. His power overshadows all other powers that can cover us if only we will totally depend on the Father God.

On July 27, 2014, from 2:00 a.m. to 3:00 a.m., I dreamed that I was preaching, and the theme was *the missing link*. With this missing link, I was explaining how we were put on the planet Earth for replenishing, taking dominion, and following his commandments to glorify him and for his pleasure. And since we got here, we behave like we don't have any overseer and came here on our own accord, doing our own lifestyles to complement ourselves instead of our master and overseer. Do we know he created us for his pleasure?

We don't even care if the things we do hurt him, and all these abominable sins we indulge are taboos in heaven. "This link is, you are my image. I have created you to live on earth as my footstool while I live in heaven on my throne. Then we work in partnership that we should like all that I like, despite me giving you your own thoughts and desires to make your own choices. They should be wise choices to include my desires too. Knowing how you got here, the package included in your creation is clearly in the Bible.

"Our partnership is guided by the Bible to enable us to trash Satan, the middleman, who doesn't want happiness for both of us. Take care of all these beautiful creations, and make accounts when my kingdom comes to the planet Earth." Then complacency sets in we take matters up and cause havoc, and instead of following His rules, we'd rather follow the rules of the enemy, making our Maker's plans not work. Have we forgotten even the great redemption through the Son of God dying that shameful death for our sake? He gave his only begotten Son. Who on earth can do this?

This link should be the link between partners in marriages, bound by the bond of "for better or for worse." Partners in businesses are to be bound by truthfulness and accountability. Also, we must love our maker with all our hearts, minds, and whole beings and love our neighbors as ourselves. Then accept the Son to purify ourselves, have faith, and believe to enjoy this earth till his kingdom comes. Majority are doing the contrary and make us miss the link, which is completely going to take some of us to hell.

Missing the link to connect to God is hell. Our redemption caused him the biggest price. And for our love, he did it anyway to pay that price as part of that security to purchase mankind. For his riches, he became poor for us to be rich; for being sinless, he became sinful for the contract to redeem us. Who can do that? Sin is the major thing that separates or widens the link between us and our heavenly Father.

The more he wants us to be guided and be obedient to him according to his commandments and statutes and manage the world back to him from the devil, then the more sinful we become and satisfy the devil like the devil created the world. How should God create the world for the devil to destroy it? He created nothing just to destroy everything, all by the chances he lures to us. The bottom line and the importance to this situation is for all of us to try and live righteously to please God as our way of being grateful for being in this world and for the owner who is ready to give us our crown. He does not want us to suffer much before we wear our crown for the good work done. If only we will be attentive, trustworthy, and obedient, his love will always protect and his grace will be sufficient for our well-being.

On August 4, 2014, from 10:30 a.m. to 11:00 a.m., I took a train to Trenton from Philadelphia with the intention of catching up with the then secretary who was just done with the secretary of state matters. I had written a letter, directed by our heavenly Father. It all had to do with the then president. I made the letter ready and attached it with some preaching that no human being should be chosen above God and that she should help me inform him. I was having a hard time reaching him, and trying to call the White House was to no avail.

Before I set off to New York that day, all the revelation is to talk to someone at the political office. I called several times to talk to the president, and when they asked whether I had an appointment or not and I said no, they did not help me book that appointment with somebody but left messages in the recording lines. Then I started calling President Clinton's foundation office, trying to reach Secretary Clinton if she can help me and never rushed.

There, too, were recording lines, and I decided to make a move by going there. Then when I reached Trenton, waiting to board another train to New York, I received a call from the Clinton Foundation to ask me my reason for coming. After relating to her, she said, "As her secretary, I can't meet her, so I can mail the letter and she will reply to me." I did and didn't get any reply up till now. I'm wondering if she received the letter or not.

On this date, I took off from work to meet madam secretary, but to no avail, even with all the messages that I was coming to meet her. After talking to her secretary, I returned from Trenton to Philadelphia and mailed the letter to her but never received any reply up till now. If she had called me to listen to me and complied with what our Father required from her, situations would have been turned to her favor. If we weigh all that is going on, it is God who chooses a leader. Yet his business is "if you take care of my business, I will take care of yours."

What was in my letter was from the Father—to do his wish, which was going to satisfy the Evangelicals to vote for her. Though she was so qualified, there was something they required from her, and I pointed it out in the letter. To their frustrations, they voted for the opponent, and I learned about sixteen million of the Evangelicals did not vote. They would have voted, and the Father would have taken care of all the intervention being mentioned day in and day out. If you chose him first, it gives the chance for him to take care of your business.

Beloved! Let us choose God first in all our deliberations because he can do what no one else can do. All power belongs to him, and we can't pretend that we are not aware of that.

I knew for sure that one woman was going to be included on the American seat just like how Margaret Thatcher was in Britain and Angela Merkel in Germany. Yet only he could change people's hearts to favor what he wants. All hearts are in his hand to turn to where he pleases. Yet everything happens for a reason, another decision for another time. Whether the first one strengthened you or weakened you in all situations, we give him the glory. He knows the end from the beginning. He would have recognized his sovereign human being.

"My daughter," he whispered gently, and I quote, "let these politicians know I gave them the charisma to win the people and also turn their hearts for those who care for me. Because they belong to me, and I want the best for them. I want them to include me since they rule on my behalf. All human beings playing any role on earth for my people, whom I have created, are playing on my stead as my partners on earth while I am also in heaven, fighting for their needs with my backing. Which parents do not care for their children regardless of any situation at stake? Parents still want the best for their children regardless of any difference.

"Fighting for their needs here on earth to make them comfortable, better lives require being mindful of their spiritual lives and where they go from here. That demands them to know the right from wrong after they have chosen the gay community. They are battling for them with meeting because they love them, then love them on earth and not in heaven. Teach them to hate sin to support what the Evangelicals tell them to make a difference in their lives, making the world a better place and living better to please me, who has chosen them to do his work here on earth. Before your conception, he knows this day will come on his behalf.

"This assignment is for the one who was created for such a time like this to change things for the better, and he will go ahead and change for me, your God, and for the people I love and for the whole world before I come to give my judgment. This will liberate many people from hell. I will forever love my people and will be fighting for their interests." As I told you, he had to get a platform and continuously echo to the world apart from the books. He asked me to do it with him up to as far as I can reach but to a suitable position, which will be beneficial to them.

I am to find a way to convince him with his backing all along. This will benefit all those practicing the abominable sin. They are all created by our Father God to be hijacked by the enemy, starting from their mentors who were equally my children as well. Some even killed those who led them into becoming that. That's why we need a platform as it's important or like a talk show to make it continuous to show the right thing to do on earth.

"All have dreams or visions to be accomplished, and I watch over my predictions to come to pass or my visions for victory. Like yourself, your mother was told in a public transport that she has a great mission to fulfill. And she didn't know what to do. You, too, did not know.

"And your teacher told you to read your Psalms at age twelve and you, too, didn't know the meaning of it. I was still watching over my word over you. Even when you refused your grandfather to convert you into his belief as a Muslim at age four, he forbade your mother never to send you to school, and I made that tenant Aunty Aggie send you to school, much to your mother's disapproval for being afraid of her father, the imam's forbidden curse.

"Then the devil whisked you to marry that man to bury your vision. Instead of coming to marry that man who was engaged to you in the United States, do you recollect the tears you shed before the marriage? That was your spirit and soul that was going to be imprisoned. And during the marriage, you could have died through childbirth and even poisoning after he used your blessing to acquire money, and I was in your midst to protect you, reading your Psalms.

"I answered your prayer for the marriage to be dissolved at age thirty-five. And at age thirty-seven, many pastors told you that you were called, but you didn't know how, and you ignored it. Yet you did very great things to my people who were in need. You sent that pastor who sent you to the mountains to be healed to the Bible school, and I whispered to you to get yourself enrolled. You did go through the studies and got your certificate and diploma in biblical principles. You still lost your ordination by coming here to help your children through colleges and childbirth since all were here in the United States. Still you are doing evangelism on social media and sharing tracts everywhere, showing how much you care.

"At age forty-six, your pastor and prophet, the overseer from your local church in your home country, confirmed this prophecy in church to you and your son that you both have calls to answer. Yet you did not answer and was doing a one on one. And in 2014, I thought it was crucial to give you this assignment, seeing your love for me. Since then, I have seen that you are very serious even now at sixty-six years old, ready for my work than in your prime age. Take courage for what is written is written and will surely come to pass," he echoed to me.

"I am reminding you all these to tell them that all have been assigned for some roles to play. Those are big, medium, and small roles. Though you might not discover or even accept it, I will still watch over you to accomplish it, never to fail to accomplish. This is happening to both of you now, like I said to Zerubbabel in the Bible that though the appointed time will tarry, it will surely come to pass. These are my security, watching over my Word and you to succeed."

On August 5, 2014, at 12:24, the bishop of my prayer line declared that there are some people on this prayer line whom God is starting to locate for them to be exposed, to come out from wherever they were hiding. They should pray for their stars to be exposed. Pray and pray. And I have been praying ever since, waiting for this time to meet the one assigned to assist him for completion. The book should be read to help the job completion through him involved.

Supposing all the people in this circle are happy, do they know what they are involving themselves in? Either they refrain and come back or become an enemy to him. If they wait till the end-time and hope we all know where we are going from here, where do we go? If we know it might benefit us or not, then make sure we are only citizens of heaven and will be leaving soon with accounts to give about our lives here on earth and how we managed them.

Chapter 17

His Acceptance

On August 10, 2014, at 5:00 p.m., our Father God whispered to me, with reference to 2 Chronicles 7:14, that if we shall seek his face and humble ourselves and refrain from sin and the abominable sin, then his wrath will subside and he will heal the land from cancers and all incurable diseases and stop all the unnecessary deaths. What is impossible to man is possible to God, like totally making the country healthy free from all unwanted tragedies. With suicides and deaths, especially among children and grown-ups, all need his protection with his people doing the right thing by staying away from sin.

On August 23, 2014, at 5:10 a.m. again, he said, "America! Wake up from your sleep. The nation that trusted in the Lord. What went wrong? Your forefathers built this nation on a solid rock and with the foundation of honoring me with Thanksgiving. What went wrong? The only one nation that celebrates Thanksgiving. They agreed to be one people, one nation, under one God and ended with 'God bless the people, God bless America.' Now blessing you and making you my eye to take care of other nations as the first nation has spoiled you and allowed you to make some attitudinal changes for the worse, grieving your loving Father who cares so much for you. Still, I love you and am fighting for you to come to me.

"Who do you think cares about you more than me? Listen! Stop the opponent who pushes you with his fallen angels, principalities, and demons on earth and in the sea with witches and wizards as his agents to do evil with the carnal man. He has nothing good for you, neither does he celebrate your joy. He robs you of your joy and then lets you think that I make you suffer. I never make you suffer if you do the right thing. For many continuous evil things, I will only rebuke and chastise you to change for the better.

"Know that the wages of sin will be death that can end you with sin to be in the fire. This is to let me know that if I blame him for rebelling and replacing you in his place for my pleasure as he was doing for me, you, too, are equally sinful. And my plan has failed. This is the cause of forever fighting between him and man. Know that every good and perfect gift is from God and that I never created you to suffer. I always want the best for you as my custodians.

"Every suffering is orchestrated by your brother, the accuser, straight from the Garden of Eden. Despite my combating, he is still on the move to enable you to hurt me. Therefore, try strongly to fight and resist him to flee. The Bible is there to guide you. Delve into it, meditate the words for your guide, and learn the Word to be used as your weapon.

"Knowing your right as a child of the Most High God with the right words, let him flee away, and only a few are doing that. Please fight his war of sins involving your body as my Spirit lives in you, meaning I live in you, and that is my first grieving sin that drives me away from you to lose my covering on this land in his domain to use you like he created you."

Listen to him, the heavenly Father. None is his equal. Put him first in all you do here on this planet Earth.

"I am your heavenly Father, who created the heavens and the earth and everything thereof. For my love to you, I made you custodians. Do you think my payback is to sin grievously against me, knowing that I abhor sin, which will never be part of me? Try to refrain from sin and affect other nations. I can't afford to lose you, so come back home to me for your party and inheritance. Just like the prodigal son, I will always love you, America, which is like my first son. Your price has been paid by my only begotten Son with that precious blood. Benefit from the blood by getting closer to me in righteousness, and it is your best bet and protection.

"He who did all things to create you should also enjoy your companionship and not that heartless, abominable, rebellious entity who is abusing the little powers he acquired from serving me on my own children. He comes to steal your body by possessing you with his agent spirits and pump you with pride to do what he wants—to destroy your body and to get you killed with the wages of sin, destroy, and then leave you to regret in sickness or to even commit suicide. Whenever he manipulates and uses your body, he wants you dead."

Just consider sin with suicidal death in this country. Nobody who commits suicide ever goes to heaven to God but to hell with Satan. You are not the owner of your body and therefore have no right to take your life just like those who kill other people. Those who do that later regret it and didn't know what happened to them and end up in suicides, which is about 40 percent among the transgender community. If they really love what they do, why do they end up committing suicide? The devil, who convinces them, has vanished to leave them to decide their fate now.

On August 25, 2014, at 11:55, praying with my regular divine prayer line and doing one week fasting, he prophesied and said there is somebody on this line who has been conceived with a big vision soon to be given birth and be promoted by God to a higher level for people to doubt whether he or she was the same person. And it will be a surprise like how David killed Goliath and how the shepherd boy cut the head of the Philistine giant. Saul could not believe his eyes. Only God can do all wondrous work. Everybody has a purpose to fulfill.

"Now the Americans are closing the peace between us to ignore the peace I have bestowed on them that surpasses all understanding and to be free from all disasters that nobody else could cause to happen."

On August 26, 2014, at 12:20 a.m., the same prophecy came with the confirmation of Isaiah 60:1–4. Knowing it concerned me, I said that I received it in Jesus's mighty name. Amen. He continued, "When the glory and favor come upon you, you can go where you couldn't go before. The same glory empowered David killed Goliath, who Jah blesses and no one has cursed. Then whatever you have lost will come back."

The same prophecy came again on February 22, 2014, at 12:21 p.m. by the same prophet that God is about to reveal for you, for America, and for your family, like how David killed Goliath for the Israeli's army saw how.

On August 27, 2014, at 11:40 to 12:20, there's another same, continuous prophecy by the bishop, quoting Isaiah 60:1–6 and 1 Samuel. "Don't let your problem intimidate you. When the time comes, you will be like Joseph, Ruth, David, and Esther, who were all born to fulfill some certain missions at some appointed times. Don't think about whatever people will say that your time is past, for God's time is the best for having accepted you as my daughter.

"Though the appointed time will tarry, it will surely come to pass. If Ruth got the second chance to marry Boaz, following Naomi, her mother-in-law, to give birth to Jersey for Jersey to give birth to David, for Jesus to come from that bloodline to save mankind, then your time is now, and I know I am talking to somebody on this line." And because the pastor from my birth country has said it before, I knew it was me who is to be located to reveal things.

I took the decision to come out of my shelter of being a caregiver in someone's residence to work on all that I have heard since I started the book already. I took notice that I was not allowed to tell people. Only in a while, I will say I am writing a book.

On August 28, 2014, at 6:30 a.m., "You see, my daughter," he prompted me, "proofed me and tell the people that that woman Joan Rivers, who ordained the homosexual marriage about three days ago, had a cardiac arrest on August 28, 2014 and let's see if she will survive. This is my sign of abhorring this abominable sin and people caring less about me and encouraging them. A woman encouraging this died from something simple in a few days. Woe betide those who are stubborn to me, knowing the right thing and doing wrong. Who is the owner of your life? To the VIP who approved for the president to follow, his son died of cancer. When I am so hurt without any remorse for longer, then these actions are against those who trashed me."

On August 29, 2014, at 10:00 p.m., "You have come to burst in the month of September. You will burst like an egg for a good course to surprise people who will never believe because you will be a changed person. You will be blessed in the world to affect your children to glorify my name as God. You might have gone through enough like disgrace, shame, and litigation. Now your world is changing for the better. There is a time for every person on earth to face persecution, to face attack, and then to excel, if only they will be obedient and recognize me as God who has an expected end for them, and put me first. Now your change is coming. Prepare for your change in Jesus's mighty name through this mission you are to accomplish.

"Your new birth is coming, like the woman who was to be stoned to death. And Jesus saved her as no one could throw the first stone for they have all sinned. And from that day, her world was changed. By Colossians 2:14, all the bad things, which rubbed you, will now be recovered, for all your debts will be covered by your Father God as a new creature. Therefore, receive your money, blessings, healing, and all you have lost." And I replied, "I receive them in Jesus's mighty name. Amen."

"And sing praises that God is doing a new thing in your life. Sing always, and it's because of your reverence, trust, and love for me."

You see, Father God prophesied through the pastor from my birth country and my prayer line prophet and is now talking directly to me and confirming them. So now I have accepted nothing but the truth of the assignment, which is crucial to be embarked on. My Father has accepted me and assigned me, so there is no time to waste. I have been so thankful to the ultimate God for what he did, has done, and will be doing. He has been with me from the womb, my childhood up to now, assigning me. So many miraculous things have happened to me, knowing these are the fingers of God to help and deliver me to live up till now that I'm not dead, being very thankful.

On August 30, 2014, at 10:00 a.m., the prophecy continued, using Isaiah 60:1–4 again. Rounding up how people will be looking for me, kings and people I did not know will come listening to me. Just like David killing Goliath, Saul asked for his father, and the women sang for him. "This will be when the glory of God comes upon you. Even your enemies will search for you."

On September 1, 2014, then later when I read Isaiah, the whole thing sounded like how God talked through Prophet Isaiah to tell the Israelites about his plans for their assignments.

"This time," he said, "can you brainstorm how I created you as a human being? From conception through pregnancy and delivery, all are mysteries. The anatomy, physiology, and others contribute to them all."

"Yes, Lord, I have also specified earlier on in this book that was genus, all found out from the doctors, as they know more from what they have seen of those mysteries."

"As such, no one is right to put that expensive spermatozoa, which produces human beings, on top of feces, an abomination to your Father in heaven, who specially formulated you. Since mothers never give up on their children, so I will never give up on you till you know and do the right things, allowing me to repeat many times to hear."

On August 4, 2014, at 9:00 a.m., "Listen, my daughter, a thorn in your flesh is something tormenting you, and no matter how hard you tried, it keeps on coming back to life. And this happens when you fail to listen or obey me, because if a good and perfect gift is from me, God, as I declared in James 1:7, then I do good things for my children who know me, are happy to recognize me, and depend solely on me and no other, for all powers belong to me.

"That was why the first man, Adam, was cursed to till the land of thorns and thistles when Satan used Eve to lure them to disobey me. Then they were later liberated by Jesus when he came to die for mankind. He was made a thorn as a crown to my Son, who came to save you, my people. When my children proved stubborn to me, I had a way of chastising them to be alert. Though I will forgive them when they pray for forgiveness, they will suffer first so as not to do that again, just like what I did to my people, the Israelites, as the apple of my eye.

"It is easy to stop all the things happening with terrorism. The world has proven to be stubborn, and you need to renew your minds like how God created people. Giving you the freedom to make your own choices doesn't permit you many unwanted sins against me. Knowing sin can separate us, so hate them.

"And therefore, we are going through all these turmoil that they can't foresee and make changes. Don't they have ears to hear and eyes to see and feel the pain of the troubles?

"Therefore, they would not have total peace until they accept me and depend on me and be obedient. You knew before you came to work for your Father as we are partners. I am aware of what you are doing in the world, trying to fight for democracy for the whole world for peace, and I appreciate that, meaning you have fully embraced me and accepted me and are doing it for me. Like I myself will do so, try and stay away from all manners of sin. I mean the ex-president and the VIP, whom I have chosen, but the ending did not please me.

"The USA and Great Britain are the world leaders and are practicing sin so seriously and are spreading it like it is something normal. Oh, my beloved people, refrain from this heinous sin," said the Lord our God, expressing some of His pains. Are we grieving him for creating us? Oh! People of God, can we put a stop to it? Are we not afraid of his creation and cherish them?

Help is on the way with advocates and prayers and fasting by all Christians as a team, working with all hands on the canoe. We can put that sinful manager to shame, and we will be obedient and go back to him. Then the Father can cause them to be at peace with the world and stop all the terrorism and many causes of the Mother Nature stuff. "I am all-knowing, and all-doing, the first and the last." He continued, "I am the Alpha and the Omega, the Creator of the heavens and the earth and everything in it." He wants us to take serious notice of things and makes me keep on repeating this many times to make sure you are reminded.

"Depend on me to do those things you cannot do, and I will guide you to do your portion and be happy with the result for knowing the end from the beginning. With anything disastrous, the background has been sin (self-interest first) instead of my interest first. I'm reminding you again, the practice of that thing is so dirty it demoralizes the human race to me—it's very disgraceful that it was being hidden by those involved. And families were ashamed until now that all the abominable practices are becoming popular, and still some commit suicide.

"Do you love the one you are hurting? As I said, love each other as I love you. Do you calculate the pain and sickness you are imposing on your naive, vulnerable neighbor and you call it love while you know it can cause problems, even death? Still I do not blame you 100 percent, just that you are vulnerable to Satan, who can use you. I am ever ready to liberate you if you will allow me. Even reading this book can bring you out of it as you feel remorse and start reading your Bible and going to church to accept Jesus as your Lord and Savior. Beloved, I am ever ready for you. Never perish for Satan, he created no human-being.

On September 30, 2014, at 6:30 a.m., that small, gentle voice was whispering to me to write all that I have jotted down together and write a book for the advocates and for those who will get the chance to read for conversion to help the kingdom. "That interview incriminated them to reverse in a way to correct whatever mistakes they made. I still love my people and selected them for the election for my people. Seeing me through them and loving the people like I myself love them, they love and do anything and overdid them.

"For the people to see me through them and how they both have their charisma to entice the people, their true love for them brought this disobedience to me. They both, the president and the vice, really love the people like their own. My love for them is unconditional but shows them the right from wrong. Only they overlooked my interest. Who is above me, God? Do you know? Tell me, can those you choose create like I, God, do?

"Putting me first, as I told you before, moves me to fight all those battles you cannot fight yourself, knowing the devil will not leave you alone, and I care. Nobody created anything but me. That creation took a lot of wisdom that only I and, I say, I alone can do that. Putting me first will let me be around you as a wall of fire and the same fire in your midst.

"They had to include me in all their deliberations by praying to invite me every morning and before you close. Purity of heart is really loving these people and living with righteousness. I should never be left out in the affairs of men, even in politics of all countries. Without wisdom, they run in circles with many mistakes. While my counseling will be available for you anytime for my people, politicians should know that I created the people, and I am also mindful of their welfare, well-being, and total happiness on my rules.

"Wisdom is better than weapons of war, and it is the answer and not claiming the precious lives of sons and daughters who mostly never left any legacy or have fulfilled their destiny. More sons and daughters have perished already, fighting for other nations. Many solutions are awaiting you. Bring your cases, and let us reason together. Many things need wisdom and prayer for settlement instead of wars that claim my precious lives. Any leader for war, think twice.

"Regardless of their sins, they are pardonable. Only resist him to flee away and be secured with me, your heavenly Father. I am always there for you more than you can imagine. I remember you in your low estate and feed all souls. All cries and prayers lead to me, even the devil himself gets permission from me before he attacks, like he did to Job. I did not allow him for his heart. Job overcame it, and all that he lost were doubled back to him to shame the devil. With my mark on you, he dares not attack you for you are covered by the blood of Jesus, my begotten Son, to pay for all your sins so you don't owe the devil anymore. The name and the blood are your covering and security for your protection. At the mention of this name, every knee bows and every mouth confesses, and the Holy Spirit's fire consumes your enemies."

The heavenly Father continues, "How many of you, politicians, will allow your children to go to wars or practice that stigma to disgrace the family? Do you care for the people you lose in wars and for the money you spent on wars? Some leaders do well to protect the people and refrain from wars, especially the recent ex-president and his administration. If I am in your midst, all things will be taken care of amicably with love and grace to bring peace and to change your negative tendencies. The world without my presence is full of chaos, and with me, there is peace.

"Therefore, make the protection, guidance, and direction of righteous living your first priority. The young and up-and-coming generations are important. Pumping wisdom into them gives best directions for their security to defend themselves against the master destroyer. They would be the barrier as our future leaders. It's not necessary to keep the truth to spoil a child who does not help after you. Though their world consists of computers and modern gadgets, they need the past too. There are pros and cons of everything. One can't be left out for the success of the other."

On September 12, 2014, at 3:00 a.m., he had reminded me again of the country and whispered, "Oh! America! The country that trusts in the Lord. Now what went wrong? Many prayed to me prior to their coming here, then they started serving Mammon, which is money and wealth, forgetting how many times they cried to me to give them the chance to come here and I did.

"After they achieved what they wanted, then they pollute the system with their pump up from the enemy, forgetting even if I am hurting, to the extent of losing themselves for him to use their bodies where I left my Holy Spirit to live inside them, to nurture them for Me. Ungratefulness is hurting. Hurting me is like your natural father, like Jesus, who is also your friend. But the Holy Spirit is rather serious and does not warrant any forgiveness. It only entails serious punishment that needs caution from hurting the gentle Holy Spirit. Don't even try hurting him.

"You know, I, God, will never let go of my beloved people. I will keep on fighting for them till the end of time, either on the mountaintop or in the valley."

On February 19, 2015, at 7:20 a.m., "My daughter, don't forget the platform to make it a daily routine, showing either you or telling the assignee what needs to be done. Keep on reminding them using that precious blood of Jesus. The lion of the tribe of Juda is the master planner who put everything in place like a project, which was enforced to come to be with a pronouncement.

Only for human beings was that clay used, like a potter molding and breathing into it for it to become a human being like his image to get a companion. He used five days to do all the things and created the first human being, Adam, on the sixth day and accepted that they were all good. That was planned. He produced and accepted that his production was perfect and rested on the seventh day of the week. Therefore, the seventh day, being Sunday, is for his praise and worship, for His service.

If human beings, who God made custodians, will cautiously examine all the creation that God created and made us the overseers, that alone will not allow us to sin and hurt him but live in righteousness to please him. Righteousness is what he so much craves from his beloved people. When they stop being sinful and will humble themselves before him, he will always forgive and heal our land, and any other country who does will be blessed.

On September 13, 2014, at 2:15 a.m., he continued, "Do you understand your shortcomings and do anything to be cautious in your life and make the right choices?" His forgiveness is always eminent. It's only that he does not want us to be sinful and do it deliberately. Doing that to your family, neighbor, or your partner still affects him since we are being stubborn and not being obedient according to all he is telling us in the Bible.

"When putting men and women to war, think about their lives and their families, those who depend on them, and their loved ones. The last thing is losing a life when all options become futile before war and losing precious people becomes eminent. Even with that, all governments should want peace, unlike before when they are aggressive just to fight, to show human powers that doesn't even last, like powers from me that need only prayer and fasting and obedience to bring peace.

"With me, God, in your midst and around you everywhere, I will turn tempers to always be amicable for settlement for peace in the world. Live with your God of all creation and miracles. Man doesn't know the strength I put in to make humans. Seek my counseling, and always pray for my help before taking drastic measures to lose the people I have created.

"The fault is when you think you are mature, sensible, and powerful to do things. Not putting me first doesn't make things easier and even makes you go in circles like all stubborn people. Make a point from today and involve Me your God in your deliberations and projects to see the difference. The children who are always at peace with their parents enjoy peaceful blessings and will affect all generations that come after them and will be called blessed. Being parents, start praying for the release of those blessings to come upon their generation.

"Grandparents are praying for parents and grandchildren. Parents also pray for children and grandchildren, and it becomes a solid foundation from generation to generation. This encourages me, God, to bless the families that pray. Because if the foundation is weak, what can the righteous do? There can be a family of ancestral curses, altars, and foundations of evil to control our lives. And those generational prayers can be breaking any holdback curses to move you forward steadily from decades to liberate that family from abominable sins.

"When it's your turn, you just continue with prayers, fasting, and acceptance of Jesus, for salvation connects me to cover your back by passing through the small, crooked way. Though not easy, it leads to eternal life to see your heavenly Father and rejoice forever in peace without tears and fears. God's people will rule in the millennium being the thousand-years kingdom of God, and his government lives without death" (2 Timothy 2:12).

Thinking of the easiest way of the world system leads you to the broad way, where the end is deadly and whose owner is Satan, who is very real with human beings, using the world system in all spheres of live and not only in gays, transgenders, lesbians, and those mentioned from the beginning. He rules in the governments to use people who have been voted there to selfishly think about themselves and their families instead of those who voted for them there.

The devil rules in the hospitals to use nurses and doctors to kill those who have no covering of God for their souls to wait for him. He rules in the pastors driven by his agenda to kill their congregations for their souls to wait for him. He rules over the youth and wherever there are people doing anything. He rules there, looking for blood as his food and souls to bring with him to hell until he is tied and released no more. He is at serious war with mankind, and we have to be alert for his tricks and combat them. We have to be vigilant.

Then comes the Judgment Day, and there will be no time to discuss your guilt and innocence. All are written in the Book of Life, just the pronouncement for your position, hell or heaven. For the pronouncement of believers and unbelievers, there will be no parole purgatory or second chance, only your accountability. After hearing your judgment, there is no turning back.

Among us would be the atheist, haters of God, the rebellious, and the religious sinners who thought they don't need Jesus but only God and the good and nice people and neighbors who don't accept Jesus Christ. Being self-righteous and thinking Jesus was for Jesus—it doesn't work like that. We go through Jesus to God by his grace and not our works. Nobody is good enough without the death of Jesus Christ on the cross, who said it was finished.

Chapter 18

Fighting for Us

On September 12, 2014, at 5:15 a.m., during the morning devotion time when we were still giving thanks to him as we normally do, the crying got into me. I could not pray; I was only crying when I started hearing him. "I couldn't afford to lose as many as you are anymore to my opponent, challenging me as my enemy. He never ever wants your happiness as I keep on telling you. I am stressing on things just like I did in the Bible the more they sin to entail punishment. I still never want to lose track of them, making me repeat my cautions several times just like now. Refrain from being sinful, and come back to me. Nobody loves you more than me, who owns your whole life and will fight for your peace and well-being since from your mother's womb and will continue every step of the way to fulfill your purpose."

On September 13, 2014, he explained with the Romans 8:1–13 and Isaiah 8:10–16, where both declare that there is no condemnation for those who walk after the dictates of the Spirit and that those who are after Jesus Christ cannot be guilty of any form of condemnation, except those who walk after the dictates of the flesh and are enslaved wanting the things of the flesh, which are all contaminated with the world's sinful nature. Walking consistently in the Spirit draws righteousness to keep you closer and closer to your heavenly Father. He knows your wants at any moment even before you come to think of them. He knows before you've asked.

He knows you want a house as a shelter, a car to be mobile, clothes in your wardrobe to keep you warm or cold, and others. He will supply all your needs at the due time according to his riches and glory in heaven if only we will make him Lord over our lives. Fighting for earthly material things in sinful ways leads you only to the enemy to capture your soul in hell. Even before that, you can lose all the people you love, like your wife and others, because everything you fought for gave you peace. Then peace will elude you later.

On September 14, 2014, at 9:00 a.m., the whispering came. "Because one relationship failed you, it doesn't allow you to go into a relationship with the same gender. It was because you did not ask me and prayed to connect you to the correct partner I created for you. But you just jumped into relationships and classified sex as lovemaking. With the devil as a witness, it will never end well but in chaos.

"Praying for the second chance will give a better answer from me than going in your worldly wisdom to create this kind of sodomy I so hated and will drive me from you. I am your God of second and many chances. Allowing me into your affairs, there is nothing I will or can't do. I celebrate you and share all your sorrows and pains. Stop stressing, crying, and being in pain. Just tell me your wants in prayers and live in righteousness and put me first.

On September 24, 2014, at 11:30 a.m., as said by the prophet, as a prophecy to someone here, the appointed time is now, with reference to Romans 9:8–15. "If that person is listening to me now, your appointed time is now." The angels told Sarah that a year by this time before we come, she will have a baby. And that son will inherit Abraham, who will be the father of many nations. God is aware of whatever you are going through. He is all set with the answers, waiting for your mind-set, growth, and maturity. Rushing from your side doesn't give you a waiting spirit. He wants to be glorified. Your time is coming as a glorification the Father himself. The glory of God is going to be manifested through your success, and the enemy hates that. That makes him cautious to figure out the time for you.

He makes things happen for many reasons. Before that, the prophet from my home country had also called on September 27, 2014, at 4:20 p.m. to prophesy, reading Psalm 91:7, that I should not be afraid, and Jeremiah 1:4–10, reading the vision that God gave to Jeremiah as the typical example he wants me to undertake. Jeremiah was sent to the Israelites, and I will be sent to the Americans just like what was specified. I should be watchful and not lose guard to do it as it has been specified as my purpose to fulfill at such a time like this. And I should be careful not to fail in any way and know that God is with me.

He had put his Word into him to go to nations. He was sending him and that he should not be afraid, that he would be with him to these kingdoms to root out, to pull down, to destroy, to overthrow, to build, and to plant. This will caution any nation or kingdom to listen and listen well to do something about it. Warnings from God himself should not to be taken easy. This shows how mankind has been stubborn since creation as God keeps on sending people until now. How long can we change for the Creator?

Sodom and Gomorrah failed to listen, and they were burned to ashes. No one was left. When God reaches his limit, punishment follows, and there is no blame game. He sounds the alarm of warning and caution just like how he is repeating many times to write in this book. The Israelites were cautioned oftentimes. You'd be amazed how many times they went back and forth, pleading, fasting, being forgiven and liberated, and going back to be sinful again and again. Similar things are being experienced in the world today, even with Christians. Instead of being remorseful to stay away from sin in its entirety, we are chastised, rebuked, and we rebuild and continue thinking we are Christians serving Jesus as the church.

If we can reflect where we read from the previous pages, this is the second time these two prophets have spoken about this agenda. The prophet continued and said Jesus demonstrated the eating of the bread as his body and drinking of the wine as his blood as a new covenant of his blood poured out for all mankind for redemption of our sins to be reconciled back to the Father. With the death and resurrection of Jesus, we have learned our lessons of doing no sin but living righteous lives. Still there has been a war between the flesh and our spirit, and we are to be aware to yield to the Holy Spirit as our choice.

Still a lot has been going on, and Jeremiah 1:4–10 confirms the way he is bringing us again to secure his people this time. This war between God and Satan has been going on since over two thousand years ago, and God is doing all within his power to recover us, no matter the cost, if we can remember the precious blood of Jesus on the cross.

Satan has been trying to neutralize his plans since we are not stable with life's encounters. Human beings had to be attentive listeners and doers—all that God uses people' to tell in prophecy, dreams, revelation, and from the Bible, taking them seriously. I myself have been facing much delay that I don't know what happened, but many distractions posed by Satan stopped me from writing this book. Yet it is my purpose that I've been assigned to complete and no matter what happens, He will help me to complete.

If I can recall, some of those distractions and of how the devil had dealt in my life to try to let me lose all that God had blessed me is with fraudulency in litigation. This never gives me peace of mind to complete this book. I hold on to my faith, seeing that God is in control to help me get them back. All the people involved in fictitiously taking what belongs to me died.

The stubborn one was found dead in his room in the morning without being sick. The other ran to Germany, and my prayer was for him to be returned. He returned and drove with the remaining two to their hometown in my home country and were all crushed to death. When God's persuasion fails on you, then the consequence happens as the wages of sin is death. For those who go to church only at Christmas and Easter, thinking they know God but don't know Jesus, Jesus, too, will not know them. The only security is salvation and baptism, and it should be now. No more time to be wasted or time of grace.

Any good father like God does not spare the rod to spoil the children. He even said it in the Bible. Hence, all that he does when we fail to live according to the things in the Bible is that he will keep on reminding us through the prophets, revelations, and dreams. Because if we live according to our knowledge, wealth, and accomplishments, which lead to the systems and wisdom of the world, this only works for the flesh and leads us to all the evil against him, committing us to judgment and hell.

Participating in impure and immoral adulterers, those participating in homosexuality, swindlers and thieves, greedy graspers, drunkards' slanderers, extortioners, and others stressed in 1 Corinthians 6:9–20 said those in these will not be part of the kingdom of God. Our bodies are the temple of God, and we should not contaminate them with any sort of thing to grieve the Holy Spirit living in us to connect us to God.

In other words, he wants us to live in the Spirit and do all the things the Spirit will prompt us to do. It will be all that God wants to depend on us and not to be so rigid with things in the world. He would have to do everything for us to take the load off our heads to give us the chance to serve him. That is what we do not understand. Fighting for earthly things end up with sickness without cure. But he has to cure every sickness to welcome you happily to his kingdom and live with him for eternity. It is all that he is wishing for us.

September 29, 2014, was when He spoke through the prophet from 1 Samuel 3:1–17, about how Samuel served his master Eli faithfully as compared to his own children letting God called him and talk to him, making Samuel his prophet between him and his people in Israel. Give your master full respect, and give him your heart to get a reward. Faithful and obedient servants are greatly rewarded, along with the beloved people who are willing to trust and obey.

Samuel was chosen as a prophet without even knowing it, having been called three times before Eli, his master, told him to respond like, "My Lord, speak and thy servant is listening," when he hears the call again. That was obedience, but between Saul and Samuel, hearing from God and interpreting to Saul without obeying, led him to lose his throne to David, who was obedient and became the "man of God's own heart." Among the two, God wants us to be like David by putting God first and being obedient and accepting our shortcomings, repenting and praying for forgiveness. He is so faithful and waits for the time to be forgiven.

We are really living contrary to this and are bringing frustration upon ourselves, trying to strive in life by our own efforts. He was to do all the hard things that might lead us into sin for us to be eased from the loads of the enemy. Obey to learn, and be power packed to command the Red Sea to be opened like Moses. Kill your Goliath (your enemies) like David, and start from being a slave to servant and then prime minister like Joseph. Start with trial, test, and proof to wear the conqueror's crown.

On September 30, 2014, at 11:00 p.m., it became obvious to write this book out of all I was jotting down. He continued, "When you get the gift of being a servant, learn to be a good servant to your master. Learn to serve God, and the people you are shepherding and directing unto salvation is doing God's work. Help the people God had put under your care. Love them and lead them to get salvation for eternity. We are just passing by. This world is just for our preparation to pass to eternity.

"Love them and don't curse them. If you curse anyone, the person will be cursed. And it is your duty to bring them to God to rejoice, not to suffer. When you bless them, they would be blessed. When they bind on earth, they will be bound in heaven. When they call for fire, fire will come like Elisha consuming Baal gods. Let them be prayerful, even to pray to open the Red Sea. And it will all be your responsibility to be a servant working for God, to be chosen for a compliment later as a good and faithful servant like all the pastors, reverends, and others."

Our accomplishment, money, and wealth are all out of his context, but it leads us to be sinful to bring sickness, suffering, and death. Knowing we will leave all these behind, while not living the right way depending on him to be dying the death he designed for us? As human beings, we are just passing as temporary residents here on earth. Living an easy life instead of a rigid lifestyle out of his plans for us is ridiculously against us. Since he knows us better, let's live according to that lifestyle he designed as suitable for us. He loves that. The ones called pastors should lead very good examples and display good examples.

Beloved, let's take life easy, and let him have his way from now on. Life is not about who can run faster and swifter but about righteousness and obedience to his rules, reigning by his statutes and commandments. Be a servant with a heart to serve your master and let God, who sees from afar, and the heart will richly bless you. *Jesus* was a master but served like a servant. Washing his disciples' feet was a typical example, even though Peter opposed it.

Joseph being righteous and refused to sleep with Potiphar, his master's wife. David did not kill Saul twice when he got the chance as someone anointed by God as a king. David accepted his sin when he slept with Bathsheba, Uriah's wife, and got him killed at the war front. When he kept it to himself, God rebuked him through Prophet Nathan. He accepted his fault, got punished, and later made it up to God and became his friend. We should learn from the examples of all these people and make it up to Him as our God, and we will be his beloved people he created and loves. He crowned all of them, and he will crown us too with grace.

On October 15, 2014, at 12:00 p.m., by the prophet of my prayer line, "The power of God is coming to you to do what you could not do before. Therefore, get the anointing to do everything—to preach, to do exams, and to get money for your ministry. What you were not doing successfully before will be done successfully now. This is the day you start doing things to prove your anointing." And I received it in Jesus's mighty name and said amen. Knowing all that I have been hearing from God confirms all that the two prophets have been prophesying were very true. I know them from the whispering and promptings he has been leading me to do.

On October 28, 2014, at 12:00 a.m., the prophecy was continued by the prophet. "God will wipe away all your disgrace and replace all that you had lost." Truly, problems have let me lose my confidence or self-esteem—to be sold while I had all my documents and lose my house fictitiously. The lawyers I hired, two of them, were all corrupt because I am here in the United States, working to support my children. The house was repaired very costly, plus lawyers' fees cost me large sums of money. This is partly because I was supposed to be preaching since 2006 and have not done it until now. I am going to do it by hook or crook today, being December 31, 2017. I have started on social media already and am building my church in my house.

Procrastination has given the enemy a chance to torment and distract me with numerous problems. One problem will not finish, and another one will be emerging. "The way to drags me into them," he said. Though the appointed time will tarry, it will surely come to pass, and whoever is called is forever called". Obedience to God gets you covered even when you don't know. Being stubborn will let you feel the pinch before you get covered to fulfill your vision. And you will be the only person created to fulfill that particular purpose from God.

The fact is, we cannot be self-sufficient by ourselves. This sufficiency lets us miss that inner-peace covenant connected by Jesus to God. Our only sufficiency is in the Lord. Refer to 2 Corinthians 3:5. We can rely on his strength and power for everything. He again wants us to have liberty instead of legalism. Liberty is emancipation from bondage. Legalism makes us read legalism into everything that the Bible says. Liberty was laid down by Jesus already.

That was why Jesus came to connect us to God by grace to faith and as a correction to the legalism and not the law. Most people and leaders hide behind the veil of rules and regulations and are not genuinely serving the Lord. On the contrary, God wants us to come to him just as we are with an open heart and an unveiled face. Moses was sent by God with the laws and legalism to teach good from wrong then live by his grace and mercy to serve.

Jesus came to pay the price and made the changes to fulfill what the same God wants for us. There we are free from the power of sin, free from manipulation and control of the wicked one, free from fear, free from comparing yourself to someone instead of pursuing your God-given destiny, free from competition, free from selfishness, free to be you, free and free at last (from Joyce Meyer's *The Everyday Life Bible*). He just doesn't want us to bother ourselves, running in circles while he is there for us.

As I was watching TV on October 30, 2014, at 6:30, a prominent man announced and declared he was gay to the shock of many. Many are trying to clear the stigma away. Yet before our heavenly Father, it will never be an abomination. He is supernatural, and whatever he declares supersedes what man decides. "Why have they been allowed to grow?" he asked me. They are really growing rapidly under this current administration throughout.

The Bible was written to guide us, and everything in it is concrete and declared until the end of time. No man can count his hair, neither can he add one day into his days. I normally cry over them and say, "Oh, Father God, forgive us. Your own people are doing this to your other creation. Don't grieve over us. Instead, fight for your precious people.

You have all the powers and a little to him to make him pompous. Can you get your powers back? Can you get those powers back to stop him from all that he is doing to your children to only hurt us?"

Lord God has won the fight to redeem his beloved people to be free from this bondage, leading us from hell. He used some judges to prove that homosexuality is not anybody's right and, as such, is illegal. That was the ruling by some forty-seven judges, and I quote from WhatsApp on April 30, 2018, as follows:

European Court of Human Rights:

> *Homosexual marriage is not human rights.* Being the judgment of the Human Rights Court of Strasbourg in France by forty-seven judges. And here it was unanimously, the World Court of Human Rights has established, verbatim that "there is no right to homosexual marriage." The forty-seven judges of forty-seven countries of the courts of Europe, which are members of the full court of Strasbourg (the world's most important human rights court), issued a statement of great relevance that has been surprisingly silenced by information progressivism and its area of influence. In fact, unanimously, the forty-seven judges approved the ruling that "there is no right to homosexual marriage." The sentence was based on the myriad of philosophical and anthropological considerations based on natural order of common sense, scientific reports, and of course, positive law. Within the latter, in particular, the judgment was based on the Article 12 of the European Convention on Human Rights. This is equivalent to the articles of human rights treaties, as in the case of 17 of the Pact of San Jose and no. 23 of the International Covenant on Civil and Political Rights.

In this historic, but not disclosed, resolution, the court decided that the concept of family not only contemplates "the traditional concept of marriage, that is the union of a man and a woman," but also that they should not be imposed on governments as "obligation to open marriages to persons of the same sex." As for the principle of nondiscrimination, the court also added that there is no discrimination since "states are free to reserve marriage only to heterosexual couples."

That is the judgment, that there are no rights for those in the practice to fight for. Lord God surprised me with this judgment when I was thinking about the conclusion. He does all things beautifully in his time. It was like I was dreaming—incredible.

When the book was almost completed, the Lord God proved himself through human beings' dealing with the worldly law to support God's claim to the hearing of his beloved people and to refrain from it without any hesitation. To prove more by the Lord God is the picture of a famous homosexual named Ardaud Paul, who enjoyed life in his homosexual practices and died with the counting rips of anal cancer per the displayed picture shown on Messenger, the common cancer that they die from. Why kill yourself like you are committing suicide? Love your life, stop the suicide, avoid hellfire, and fight to go to heaven. These are the evidences that God has won the case. It is evil but not right for any fight.

Chapter 19

Joining Jesus

Then the gentle voice came. "My daughter, write everything down. You see how humanity has treated me? I took my time to create my children, and Satan uses their bodies for such a heinous sin, and it is now spreading, not thinking even about the punishment attached to them. He has intentionally made them rich to puff their shoulders up, thinking they have money and being legalistic in fighting for the right of equality." So what rights do humans get before God? Then why don't they fight to live forever? Do they read the Bible at all? Refer to Leviticus 18:22–23 and continue to verse 30, which talks more of other sins he abhors.

The original plan of creating us in his image is being Jesus's look-alike physically. That we have a spirit that never dies. We can think, reason, and solve problems with our intellect just like God. We can rationalize to give and receive love, and we have consciousness to know right from wrong to make us accountable to God. All people possess the image of God. Either believer or unbeliever, we are all his children with his Spirit living in us to reflect God's glory like Jesus Christ. That's why we should not commit murder, abortion, or other sins and live in holiness with his power as our qualification to join Jesus and reign with Christ in the last days, the second world, or the world to come.

"Be convinced to read the Bible yourselves to know that Satan and his fallen angels are his agents. Spirits of wicked places of darkness, principalities, demons, witches, and wizards are at war with the people of God, making them very stubborn to listen to just simple logic. Be obedient with my Word and rejoice, receiving all that you want with no hustling. The agents manipulate them to do what Satan wants. Who created humanity? Can Satan do the creation of all that they are enjoying? Logically, they are to balance themselves.

"Many have read the Bible to get the clue to fight and overthrow them. Being the Creator, it affects me to lose them, and I care. He only wants their souls into the fire. I have been saying oftentimes to write them down, for them to listen and renew their minds. When they get to know, they can change for their safety to enable them to join Jesus as their coheir." He is ready with the mansions he promised that he was going to build for us all.

Joining Jesus should be embraced now. The same Jesus was the Word, who was God the Son and was with God during the creation. When Satan tricked the first man, Adam, through his wife, Eve to eat the forbidden fruit, they lost the Garden of Eden, which was purposely created for them to keep and live there. Then they were driven out of Eden through disobedience, played by Satan as serpent, leading us to be separated and fall short of his glory and driven to till the land to suffer for being disobedient. Now who was to be sent for the correction to bring God's children back?

Jesus again became the second Adam, and pay the price with a shameful suffering and death to liberate us. When he has risen from the dead and was supposed to go to the Father, he allowed the Holy Spirit, who can be divided, to be in everybody everywhere at the same time, to be with us when we are led through salvation by accepting him as our Lord and Savior. Jesus, in the form of the Holy Spirit, now will nurture us to put God first, still living in us for the best. Yet the enemy is continuously in our way. The time is up for us to live right and prepare to meet Jesus, who is about to come soon for our conqueror's crown.

This book is all about the preparation and meeting Jesus to reign with him and be for God since we belong to him and not Satan. Jesus, the soon-coming king, is almost here. Be ye prepared to meet him.

On November 18, 2014, at 5:10 p.m., I called the prophet to tell him about my son's dream about me. Before I could speak, he said there was a death before me, and he prayed to cancel it. And my son also dreamt that I was dead and laid in state; that was why I called the prophet, even though we both have prayed to cancel it before I made the call. At about 5:50 p.m. on the same day, the other prophet also called from my home country to tell me the same message and said the devil is a liar, and prayed to cancel any evil intention of the enemy, knowing I have a mission to accomplish, he was fighting to disrupt, and God is all powerful.

The Almighty God will forever protect me and all his children if only we will yield and listen. He loves to. He had protected me enough already. That is all he is doing, if you do get closer to God. Or else Satan will not allow you to finish what you were brought here to do. There are enchantments and divinations under the sea and on earth against all of us, never to complete our purpose, making our closeness, obedience, and righteousness very crucial.

His protection over us is twenty-four seven unaware. That's why we are compelled to depend totally on him. On November 22, 2014, the bishop said that whoever was having a death trap before him or her, God said it will be cancelled in Jesus's mighty name. Amen. Before that, I had declared fasting with all my children, backing it with some Psalms 91 in the morning, 16 at noon, and 35 before bedtime. They had already lost their father and wanted me to live longer to reciprocate all that I had done single-handedly for them to be on their feet.

On November 27, 2014, being Thanksgiving Day, I thanked God with my family for all he had done to bring us this far and prayed for continuous protection and deliverance for all of us from the property litigation and any predicament the enemy is always harassing us with. A distraction to complete this mission and start preaching. Since from my childhood till now, I have been really pursued by the enemy, but God will never give him my soul as I continuously tighten my relationship with him. And we should all do that for his love.

Along the line, I do some vows and share it with my pastors and the prophets. Those who spread the good news are being maintained by those who receive the good news; that is the job they do. Those who chose to work for God chose a good work. They represent God on earth, pray, and give directions to his people. I also pay tithes on leasing my house and shared for my country church and about three churches here, including Gospel for Asia on November 30, 2014. To sponsor evangelism, my passion is how people will live righteously and make it to heaven instead of hell. God loves to meet us all in heaven.

Those who know the Bible declared that gay couples should be given the chance to serve in the church. With that announcement, I wanted to hear something from God. I heard nothing. I guess he was fed up and that my heart was broken too. Why should the very people who read the Bible and those who see this declared in Leviticus 18:22–24 and 1 Corinthians 6:9–10 and others also contradict what God is saying? Why are they very serious with the "I Am the I Am"? Are we not taking things for granted now? No! We shouldn't, for He is very serious with his Word. He is not a man to lie or born by a woman that he will say and not do it.

Catholic churches have been sued many times for sexually assaulting Mass servers, contributing to the origin of homosexuality. When the boys grow up, they think it is a normal thing to do, being their mentor. The people they were looking up to were rather helping to breed homosexuality, including other mentors like fathers, uncles, head coaches, and others. With the assertion of saying they should be allowed to serve in the churches, does it mean he supported this from the beginning or what? Instead of speaking for repentance, he spoke his feeling. So how are we thinking and valuing God who abhors all grievous sins?

Feelings and emotions are not from God. Our thoughts are the origins of all troubles since many times it causes troubles from our own desires, feelings, and disobedience to him. "Your thoughts don't matter. I am of the whole universe." Therefore, we are to choose our thoughts in light of the Word of God. Knowing that, his are the best. Satan cunningly sets us up with wrong thoughts into his strongholds in his area of bondage to be able to incriminate us into suffering. He's always roaring to get a victim to consume their blood. Beloved, we should be cautious and careful with our thoughts, knowing we belong to God.

Examine what is in your mind carefully before you release your thoughts. God talks to us from the Holy Spirit through discernment and promptings or whispering. And those thoughts are beneficial to our souls and spirits to nourish us. God the Father, God the Son, and God the Holy Spirit consented into making a man in their image of the Trinity, the image of God. They love us 100 percent of the time and will do anything for us, like protection, deliverance, sheltering, clothing, and more if only we will trust and obey to enjoy his comfort and grace.

January 4, 2015, at 9:50 p.m., was when I was asked if I can get ahold of his beloved son, the past president, to complete his assignment with changing the situation of healthy and righteous living to make it up to the majority who are contemplating and worrying, and for him to complete the assignment he took charge of. He did his better. Correcting that situation will change from better to the best before him and before the world, especially those who love him.

They could have won if all things were perfect, but they lost the lovers of God—those who put God first and left them no choice. I was directed to write letters to draw their attention, but they could not be reached. Or they received them and paid no attention, making unfavorable things happen. Now the world is watching. We should pray for God's deliverance to avoid anything horrible to happen to claim American lives. For his love, he will always listen. If we could keep on praying as a nation for his forgiveness and mercy, he will listen. He always gives second chances. God, knowing well about our weaknesses and strengths, wants us to depend on his grace for our sufficiency.

Waiting! We don't have much time to wait. It's not funny. All that has been said in the Bible as the end-time is really going on among us, and many of them are unbelievable. With the revelations and many dreams among the people around the world, Jesus is saying he is coming and is showing signs of those going to hell or heaven, saying those going to hell are more than those going to heaven. Christians are specified to be alarmed.

The meaning is, God is for us and Satan is against us. Now our question should be: Are we going to live for God or for Satan? The answer is simple. Who will choose the one who is against him or her? And sometimes, Satan works through people in the spiritual realm. You will see people hating you or diverting you out of the course to do the right thing. Instead, you will indulge yourself in all the sins, like adultery, idolatry, sexual immorality, gossiping, backbiting, stealing, greediness, unforgiveness, hatred, and many more, which ends one in hell. Reference from Galatians 5:19–21 said we couldn't be a part of his kingdom.

On the contrary, our Father is not resting at all. He is showing many signs and telling children to repent and live by the promptings of the Holy Spirit, whom he left for us to convict and alert us not to head in the wrong direction and to counsel us of right directions. Then he becomes our companion and comforts us. Jesus promised he will never leave us as orphans. This is to guide us unto righteousness and live in the Spirit solely for God and not to contaminate our bodies with sins.

Living for the Holy Spirit leads to the fruits of the Spirit, which are love, joy, peace, patience, kindness, faithfulness, forgiveness, meekness, humility, self-control, and others to carry you with your good works to join Jesus in heaven. The mansions are still waiting instead of the furious fire. The bottom line is to choose lives according to getting wisdom from the Creator. On February 13, 2015, at 3:00 a.m., my eyes opened to pray, and I slept again.

Then the whispering started. "Oh! America, the country that trusts in the Lord. The country I chose like Israel. Now they have turned their backs on me. Majority of them are not living for me but are mostly living greedily on money and sins. Who can even add one hair to their hair? Rather they have polluted the world with this forbidden sins, and others are growing. Satan is still seriously polluting their bodies that I created, not him.

"Yet never will I let them go either in the valley or on the mountaintop. I will always fight to redeem them. Yet they never think of their friendship Jesus brought between us and turn it into an intimate relationship, talking to me constantly and thinking of making me smile through their true love, obedience, and trust, like trusting your human father to care for you. I am more than that. A father within fathers, a father who never leaves but waits for you to complete."

On February 19, 2015, at 7:20 a.m., "If you couldn't get him to include this in his foundation, you get a platform in the form of a talk show and echo to the world to stop those abominable sins immediately. They should start making use of the death of Jesus. I need all my people to myself. The death of Jesus forgave their sins, and they are forgiven. I need them—the politicians, the rich and the poor, the middle-income people, babies, and the youth, everybody—to live for Me alone. I don't share my glory with anybody, as jealous as I Am."

Love him with all our hearts and understanding to direct our paths with his goodness, mercy, loving kindness, protection, deliverance, and security into heaven. But having lived for the Spirit is the Holy Spirit living in you, and it's God who is living in you, so you will increase in faith, without fear, since Jesus suffered for us. Honor is ours already with God. We need to surrender all our gifts, like talent, family, career, thoughts, attitudes, desires, and money. He wants to be involved in every area of our lives to lead us into righteousness. He alone is looking forward for us and is covering our back, working behind the scenes for our interest. This is to let us know and depend on him, not otherwise.

In my case, I had been told to have a call since 1994 when I was in my shop in my country by many pastors. My answers were, "How can I be called when my mother even has a Muslim background?" Though I refused to be one of them, later I found out that I was called to bring the Muslim family to Jesus. I went to the Bible school and wanted to continue to theology, and I heard this: "Let me teach you. It's better you learn from me directly." Coming to the States, I wanted to come here to assist my children and continue from here, sharing tracts and doing outreach programs for the churches I joined. I was mostly working instead in full-time ministry.

I just worked, and all were occurring to me from hearing from him and writing all these until March 15, 2015, to March 17, 2015, where, for several times, he was now intervening for me to quit my job and resume his work. It has been enough of a postponement that he prompted me on August 2006 and June 2014. On August 2006, He had let my head pastor, the Prophet, called me and my son before all the church congregation and revealed our calls to us. I have been sharing tracts and doing evangelism on some of the Social Media with over thousands in the group of friends of Jesus and my Inspiration, leading them into salvation baptism and righteousness, the most important of all is to prepare for Jesus to eternity.

He wants me to start big with such messages to all nations; hence, this book. I had left my kind of shift since I kept on going back and forth on my resignation. I am relating my case because we have not relied on Him as what he is requiring of us. And most of the time, we do our own things and lean on our own wisdom of the world's system, which is of Satan and full of frustration. Until finally I injured my wrist at work and could not use it again. Now I am speeding up to finish, thinking we know better. Out of tragedies, we stop.

His control of us to access our transition and join him is by obeying the heavenly system. That is to be a Christian who can bear fruits by following his instructions and going by his teaching and statutes concerning the promises laid for us in the Bible. Then we exercise our faith and grow in knowledge and self-control and practice godliness, mainly of Christian love as lights shining in the darkness. Love one another, and prepare to give a helping hand to as many as you can when the need arises. Never pass by anyone suffering like it doesn't concern you because he or she is also a beloved child of God. Be ever ready to help and win souls.

God is light, so are Christians who are living in righteousness to pay close attention to shine in the darkness, which is of this world, and Christians portraying the love of God. In loving others, it is making us the real children of God, confirming that we are in the light of the world to use his beautiful creations but not of the world. This means we should not love the things in the world because we will be passing away and will be leaving them back. We came naked and will be going naked. Nothing at all is going with us that we should know and worry less.

Rather, we should love the people in the world, with us honoring the commandments that He told us. We would love him with all our hearts and love our neighbors as ourselves and bless them with the things we have. That was why He said, "I will bless you for you to be a blessing unto others." That was God's plan, rich people and majority of the stars also do that. Those who do that never lack anything from God, including paying of tithes.

He again said, "I will bless you, pressed down and shaken down together that there will be no room to contain them," since all monies belong to him—God. Being a blessing, being passionate, and being empathic with the less fortunate ones bring God's heart much to you. Especially adding righteousness to it, it makes you the apple of his eye, giving all that you desire. Reading the Bible and meditating on his Word is great, but being mindful of his people and their needs is what he cherishes the most as we share his image and are his partners.

Then you add paying your first fruits and your tithes to allow Him to rebuke the devourer and open windows heavens of mercy, favor, loving kindness, and grace for your whole life's encounters for easiness. First fruits are your very first Salary of the year. You can give all to your church without taking a cent out of it as your way of honoring God and His church.

Tithes are 10 percent out of your whole monthly salary—either weekly, biweekly, or monthly. Tithes allow more food in the church to take care of the pastors and those working in the church and other needy ones. And if you can also help in any activities in the church, this allows you to enjoy the natural beauty of the world and not pursue the things in the world to distract you; rather, you pursue your love for God and the things of his kingdom. Since it is about him, his people, and his kingdom, we are being managed by the Father, the Son, and the Holy Spirit.

The Trinity, after the initial creation in the Garden of Eden, did not enjoy the agenda for their creation through the serpent leading them to fall and be driven out of the garden.

That was their mission that was not accomplished. So as wise as they are, the Son came down to the humans' level to be the sacrificial lamb to pay that heavy price on the cross. Then the Holy Spirit took over from the Son to make sure to live in us with our salvation to counsel us to do the right thing, to live in righteousness, and to strengthen our relationship without falling again.

For their pleasure, smile and glorify for their mission to be accomplished this time around.

Chapter 20

Living for the Father

The questions for us mankind are the following:

1. Who brought us here?

2. For what reasons were we brought here?

3. Are we aware that our anatomy, physiology, etc. are the same and that we have the same blood, tendons, veins, muscles, and others with other forms of human beings of different colors?

4. What are our obligations as partners on this planet?

Then we should ask ourselves these individually: What are our lives here? Do we see things as the devil sees, or do we see them from a different perspective? Do we see life in general from God's view? The way we see our life individually will help guide us how we value our relationships, how we invest our time and money, and how we use our God-given talents to fulfill our purpose here on earth. We should see and evaluate our lives from God's perspective.

To me, my life is a journey of trials and testing, of proving that in our transit, we qualify to eventually live harmoniously in eternity with our Father in the next world. To some, life is partying and having fun;

to another, life is about expressing oneself through their wardrobe, wearing the nicest of jewelry and clothes to show off to society, having flashy cars and houses, and so on. Whatever your worldview of life is, it is like a battle. Sometimes it's easily won; sometimes not. Your life, through the wisdom of this world system, might lead you to base your life on faulty life encounters that do us more harm than good and is full of risks.

The purpose of our lives, as laid down by God in the Bible, are the only ones to help us fulfill our life's purpose meaningfully both here and in heaven. God is challenging us to replace the wisdom in the Bible with the conventions of the world. That's why He said, "Do not be conformed to this world but be ye transformed by the entire renewal of your mind" (Romans 12:2), mainly reminding us concerning the use of our bodies.

The Bible gives us three teachings from God's perspective of life. They are life as a test, life as a trust, and life as an assignment for us as partners to give accounts of what was given to us to keep, enjoy, and take care of until the king or the owner comes back. Our characters are the stories in the Bible, who guide us to be tested in faith, obedience, love, integrity, and loyalty. Again trials, tribulations, and temptations are for our refinement, like gold and silver that's perfect for our transition. Knowing our weaknesses, Jesus was sacrificed by God to come and pay the price for the propitiation of sins and give the proper foundation on earth.

Typical examples of our ancestors who were first tested were Adam and Eve, who failed in the Garden of Eden. Our father Abraham was asked to sacrifice his only heir, Isaac, to weigh Abraham's love for God. Jacob was tested to work seven more years for Rachel to become his wife. Instead of her, Leah, her older sister, was given first to fool Jacob, like how he fooled his brother, Esau, for his blessing. Ruth, Esther, Joseph, and Daniel all passed their tests. And let's not forget King Hezekiah, who was given fifteen more years, having lived faithfully before God. Yet they all passed with God's love and mercy.

We do not know the test for us individually, but everyone has a test to go through that we must prepare to pass the test for our crown. God watches how we respond to conflicts, problems, illnesses, successes, disappointments, and even how we handle people with respect and politeness at all times. I have encountered so many tests that I don't know which one to mention first. The lesson I learned is, they made me grow and mature to use my test to counsel others that if you survive them, then that person, too, can survive with your advice. Seeing life as a test gives you the courage to face them, knowing you will overcome them with God behind the scenes—He who never stops supporting you because he knows your strengths and weaknesses.

When we knowingly or unknowingly contaminate ourselves with this world's sinful values, we commit spiritual adultery, termed by our God, that is, going our own way despite knowing we are not here by ourselves. These make us live against God as enemies and rather represent our adversary, Satan, instead of God, who created us. That makes us live on earth as a temporary place and rather lose our heavenly abode with the Father.

We all know that we are created in His image and likeness—to be fruitful, to multiply, and to replenish the world. We have dominion over all that he created. We are in charge of feeding them and keeping them safe for our Father, like one who is inheriting a father's or mother's legacy. Doing what is right and proper will benefit us and our children. In other words, doing things haphazardly will let you reap unfavorably. Righteous living will be rewarded with rich, eternal life by our Father—to live in a world without tears, pain, sickness, and stress and to go to paradise with Jesus to rest.

He created us to fill the earth, like how we are now with over 6.4 to 7.5 billion people today. The reason was because the then Lucifer, the most handsome among all of God's angels who also praised and worshiped the Master, rebelled against God to claim his throne and to be like God. We were created to take his place and have leisure with

God. Someone to replace him, Lucifer, to make God happy, as His heart was broken by Lucifer. We are to be Lucifer's replacement.

Replenishing the world required marriage and reproduction, thus requiring him to create Adam and Eve as a helpmate of Adam in the form of marriage. This was the first relationship God created, which, apart from taking dominion over all His other creations, was also for union and fellowship with God because two are always better than one. When one gets cold, the other can keep the other warm. When two meet, He is always in their midst. And that relationship was supposed to be a very healthy and faithful one.

Therefore, our awareness should be on the day we have accountability to give to him. God, who has all the wisdom, created three colors, being white, yellow, and black. There were no differences in the blood, anatomy, biology, and physiology; and the doctors are aware.

I don't think that in organ transplant, we use white organs for white people or black organs for black people. They are all equal; only color, height, looks, and personality change from country to country. Christians are very good in embracing that we are all equal before his eyes, and even in churches, you can see and feel that there is no discrimination.

That makes the Infinite Father ultimate and sensible. During his creation, man was the last one he created, and he said they were all looking good because he had created them—*all beautiful in his own time.* Who are you, a mere perishable man to differentiate what the immortal God had created? The result is what we are all facing today. When we think we know better, worse things get us into frustration. Who thinks he knows better than God?

A Supernatural Entity who is omnipotent, omniscient, and omnipresent brought us here on this planet Earth to live for him as his partners and for his pleasure and be custodians of all his beautiful creations and give accounts to him. He told us to multiply, replenish, and have dominion over all his creation. To replenish humankind is to multiply by a healthy relationship—a man marrying a woman for procreation to populate the world, which is now increasing to about 6.4 billion.

How can abominable sins increase people to cover earth? If all were homosexuals, who will give birth to the children? Adoption did come so early. Children born by the opposite sex couldn't give them better lives and allow those who are capable to give them better upbringing by another opposite sex. So what will be the training from the same sex? This will be against God's creation. Just think about the kind of children brought up by a same-sex marriage.

Marriage is for union, fellowship, and replenishing the earth, as well as uplifting each other when needed. Therefore, God is for us; he is who we have to depend on, rely on, trust, and obey. It's for all that he had planned for us to work properly without any deviation. Satan is against us, only tricking and enticing us with sins to our doom. If God is for us, then it doesn't matter what other people feel about us. That is always from the devil, who lured us to the practices that normally kill those involved with cancer on the anus and AIDS. Nobody can survive to be against those who surrender to our doom (Genesis 19:4–8; 9–25).

He knows that his work on us is always in progress to perfection, which is the reason why we should trust and obey 100 percent of the time. Turn not to the left or right to enable him to fight all your battles and give you what is needed. He knows your needs more than you yourself. Your needs will be easy if you allow him to take care of you after you surrender. After my divorce for about fifteen years, friends and families were bringing me refrigerators, televisions, and microwaves without me asking for them. Anytime I see any of them getting older, he prompts others to bring new ones to come. He knows before you see; only choose him and his kingdom first for all things will follow. The world becomes easier and comfortable with him, regardless of the opponent's devices.

Anytime something good comes to you, it's him who gave the chance. Since he lives in us in the form of the Holy Spirit, he thinks with us, plans with us, supplies all our needs, and provides money to get that car, that job, that house, that clothing, and all the things that make you complete and fulfilled. He knows of them before they even occurred to you and gives them to you at the right time for your comfort and happiness, for you to be at peace and to go to church to serve him.

Our happiness is his priority, for joy, love, thanksgiving, praise, and worship prepare us until we all meet in heaven when Jesus comes. When living for God, who can be against us, nothing can separate us from his love. No eyes have seen and no mind has heard what he has prepared for those who love him. And he wants us to know that he is constantly doing new things in our lives. It only takes us to pray more, read our Bibles, meditate on his Word, and just leave every damn thing under his care. He has all the strength, all the power, and all the wisdom to make us accomplished. And Lord God wins all the battles and fights for us always anywhere anytime, if you only allow him to totally come into your lives. Though the enemy will try but never succeed, keep on praying, praising and believing.

He will be moving us forward steadily till we reach our destination. God is always good. Living on our own thoughts and understanding is not depending on our heavenly Father. That is totally of the world, and lovers of the world are enemies of God. Taking that into account, I was first told I had a calling in 1996, which I didn't even believe. In 2003, I fell sick, and nothing was detected medically. Then one young pastor took me to a very high mountain in my home country to have an encounter with God on my behalf. The mountain was like over a one-hundred-story high building with a flat top. During the night, all was cloudy; all pastors and those who want anointing or healing go there to pray. There I was told by the young pastor David to answer my calling too. I received my healing and came back with all vim to start, but I needed to get full knowledge by studying the basics of biblical principles, which he will be glad if we could study the Bible for the full understanding of his wisdom on our upkeep.

Spending three days with intensive fasting and prayers, Jesus healed me before we even returned to the city. In a month's time, a prophet who had now got a gift of prophecy asked me to help him with enrolling at the Bible school of which I did not hesitate to send him to my church's Bible school under the International Central Gospel Church that I started in 1988 when I was born again. The Living Word Bible School of Ministry now might be a Bible college.

On reaching the Bible college with the prophet David with the consultation, I heard a gentle, still voice telling me to enroll myself too. Though I did not have the money for both of us, I asked for a payment plan for both of us with the help from my children here in the States. We both started in August 2003 to 2006.

The amazing thing, I did the certificate and the diploma within three years. He did six months and left to get married. I could not convince him to complete that course on biblical principles. Having seen how he fasted and prayed for the anointing over there on the mountaintop, though marriage is not bad, I encouraged him to complete it first. It was terrible that I could not convince him. How badly he wanted to go to Bible college. He had the anointing but needed the knowledge of biblical principles, and church planting.

I went alone to complete it and graduated in June 2006. He was proud of me. I expected spiritual confirmation from the head pastor, a prophet who threw his coat on me for anointing during healing time. Again, he called me and my son in the same year to answer our calls. Preparing for ordination, I followed another church that does crusades for about five crusades in a year, including the Central Prisons for some experience. Waiting for the months to pass by for this ordination, I rushed to the United States to help my daughter on the birth of my granddaughter in 2008, having filed for my green card. Each time, there was something crisscrossing my ordination over there in my home country. Yet whoever is called is forever called. Now I am seriously into it, yearning to be on fire for Jesus, only God calls and assign His divine work.

The point I am making is, since I was first told to be told 1996 that I had a calling, have still not started my church though I have been doing one-on-one with tracts and evangelism on social media. I should have been established by now and adding crusades. Even the writing of this book alone has taken me about four years, which shows that I am doing more of my own things than what he has required of me. Procrastination too is a sin, especially with God. Let's obey Him immediately He talks to you.

My other consolation is to build his church inside my new project. I wanted my house to be called the House of the Lord as part of my appreciation for the many things God has done for me and my children out of love throughout our lives. When my ex-husband left us with all the money we had for a new woman, later he confessed and apologized before he passed away, being proud of how far God has helped us. Woe betide the people who think money is the answer. No! Jesus is the answer to all our problems.

That continues to happen to many people—starting things they never finish. Only to our disadvantages before that of God, and that delays our life destinies. Yet we should not worry. Nothing is too late to switch to him. He is still working on us to perfection. In this way, our perfection from his approval will not delay our benefits. He celebrates us. Be sure that whatever he created us for has been accomplished to make God and man both happy to the shame of our adversary. Therefore, let's put him first priority in all that we do.

I will be glad if all Christians can do their work well as the kingdom's partners to draw our people in the world to join us. As true Christians, we don't have to ignore our daily reading of the Word of God and meditation, especially first thing in the morning, to renew your mind against evil thoughts and fears. Daily secret prayer gives your life breath or you become a prey to Satan's network that the world is constantly displaying. Talk less and concentrate more on the Word for spiritual empowerment. The Word is the food of the Holy Spirit that lives in us to counsel, comfort, and accompany us for power to live for God and also intercedes for us in times of our weakness.

A Christian should surround himself with praying brothers and people that desire more of God to boost you and also with your appetite for more of God. We should not speak evil of others or envy the grace of God on others but praise them and bless them for you shall reap what you sow. Love all, and do the works of love by paying evil with good. Your example will let all men know that you are a true Christian. Run from hypocrisy; don't present yourself to others in falsehood and hypocrisy never grows in grace but grows in guilt. Never exalt activities for God above your personal fellowship with God. Many say they are working for God but are not working with God, will be ending with great disappointment.

Cry to hear from God continuously, for Christ (as our shepherd) and us (his sheep) hear his voice continuously. Try to reach a perishing soul with salvation to put a smile on Jesus's face by winning a soul. Never exalt or praise yourself; there are spiritual eyes watching your motives of doing things. Saying things about yourself gives others room to talk about you. Lead other Christians to live by these examples, and pray to stick them to live for our Father in heaven.

Time is running out. Jesus's coming is imminent. Let's strip our old nature and put away those things conforming to the world. Rather, put on your new nature created in God when you accept Jesus as your Lord and Savior and receive your salvation, making you a new creature with all sins washed away, to lead you to you reverencing him of true righteousness and holiness. With a fresh mind and spiritual attitude that helps you activate your life in line with God's Word and his will leads you to the right action with the enablement of banishing those wrong thoughts that lead you to wrong actions.

He uses the people who are depending on him with their tender and wise hearts, tender conscience, and perfect heart to avail himself to be used. Then the devil's plan can never stop God from using those who are called or anybody to be used for others. The Father calls us to love and value other people like ourselves instead of hating and devaluing them.

How is it then that about two thousand children are taken from their mothers to suffer? That one evangelist said it was disgraceful and has no biblical point of view. And does it not resonate to us American people who have shown love and care for the world over? Can we all be careful to care about human beings as our Father asked us to do? And allow the Father's Day of 2018, Sunday, show a good example to the world as good American leaders?

Before Jesus left, he taught us to love one another as he had loved us, and he still loves us. Looking after the interest of one another, being in the Lord means you have to shine in your neighborhood and your society to attract others to God. We all have jobs to do and an accountability to give to please God the Father, the Son, and the Holy Spirit. He rebukes us whenever we faulted so as to make sure we are refined for these accounts.

During the transition in January 20, 2017, with that gentle, still voice, he said, "I choose the ex-president and his vice, who are humble and passionate with love for the people, to see me in them by their charisma that they will do anything for my people. But the others obstructed them all the time till they were frustrated to even spread all over the country homosexuality, much to my disappointment and to the disagreement of the Evangelicals, who had no choice but to choose the current president, who amazingly has no political or governing experiences but might agree to their choice."

And this will really affect the other side of their choice, sinking them. And the losing side will also think twice by considering good choices in their subsequent decisions. What is the new president going to do about his dislikes, like homosexuality and gun violence? "Such are part of my dislikes, and what happens next will be to know the difference between them both.

"The attack made on the legacy of the outgoing president is not biblical to show nothing of any black president as the American president. To prove it wrong is the reason why I, the Lord God, am sending the biracial woman as a princess into the royal monarchy of Great Britain on May 19, 2018, to show that I do not discriminate against my own colors' creation and handiwork. The attack on immigrants struck almost all efforts that the past president put in place. Now the American people will know the difference."

Many things might not be understood, but it is subject to pondering, regardless of our sins. He hates to see us suffering.

There will be a difference between both presidents, but only God will know the difference. When people sin enormously, punishment will come in diverse ways. He has all the answers now. People will be battling in their minds and may not understand. Did I omit a mistake in creating man in three colors? Father God whispered to me to write down why people complain about his creation. "The colors I, God, made reveal each other's beauty. All colors are beautiful."

His agenda of affecting the historical capital of Jerusalem was welcomed. Yet many things are going on in diverse ways to the amazement of the majority. And that will affect his side somehow, and it has started, unless things change for the better. Americans should be careful to pray for intervention to avoid any future war where people may die. The country built by immigrants should not suffer in anyway but rather has the right to be screened and to repatriate the bad ones back to their birth countries, as assumed by our God: "All souls are mine and to eat."

Apart from that, what are the Evangelicals saying about the children crying against gun violence or about the zero tolerance immigration policy that is punishing innocent children who are being separated from their parents? This has been a very serious scandal on the month of June 2018, which disgraced us in the eyes of the world. The parents can face the law, but the children are to be protected. Thank God he signed Executive order on June 20, 2018, to reunite the children to their families. About two thousand or more children should be liberated.

"Although this country was of immigrants to take care of families as I, God, has made America like country of refuge, other uncomfortable things are all happening now to make many unhappy but have no choice. When my people are happy doing what is required of them, I am also happy. Because when they are in trouble, they cry to me as my people. So I love those who make them happy in the right way and it make me happy by letting them do the right thing in my eyes. Righteousness and honoring me keep us going.

"That will be our payback to live over sinful indulgences of burying facts over reality, concerning colors like I, God, have made a great mistake. Enslaving people from their birth country to use them in wars and bridges and all the hard work, now your hands are tainted with their blood. This country is like a big tree. All birds come to feed on it. And those killings of the immigrants as if the land is theirs, what should the Red Indians say?

"Serious judgment is coming upon all the killers of innocent blacks and those blacks who also kill themselves and others. None will escape my judgments as I am the judge of all rules.

"The killers will answer Me plus the instigators. You are all my people and have the right to live on my land if only you get the entry chance and follow that country's security regulations. Majority prayed to me for their visas, and I answered them before they came to live here. Racism is not of God but of Satan, along with the faultfinders through thoughts of evil intentions. Can any killer create a human being? Their hands are tainted with their blood (Isaiah 59:3) and are seriously going to answer to me on Judgment Day and end up in fire.

"Then why the discrimination like I, your God, am mistaken in my color choices? You make me feel awful for grading this as sins upon your lives and for thinking you know better than me. Do you say the potter is wrong and the pot is right? Sin upon you." Whenever a nation becomes so sinful and reaches its peak, God has a way of punishing that nation, like how the Israelites were given to nations like Babylonia and others. America has now given up to experience the difference in the two rulers. Our heavenly Father hates complaining.

Many would not understand, yet he is the president. He gave Jerusalem the capital to make the Israelites happy on May 9, 2018, which is biblical, but he withdrew from the Iran nuclear deal to bring war between the two nations. Despite that, the Evangelicals chose him while we don't see many of his policies conform to those in the Bible. I did not hear much about him being the choice from God. We, the people, can pray for him to do things to suit us. God is for us. If God is for us and we do his wishes, then nobody can be against us as he will listen to our prayers.

Having been asked by our heavenly Father to explain all that is written, know that the decision is ours to make. We were created and predestined to enjoy the garden and live forever. Then we were led by the devil and lost our inheritance. Then he recreated us in Jesus Christ to reconcile back to God with salvation by grace through Jesus. Our country needs to start taking the National Prayer Day on May 3, 2018, and each should be serious and even add some fasting for the forgiveness of sins.

We know our shortcomings on rules, regulations, and commandments laid down as guidelines for us to get closer to God. Yet easy living and living carnally for the flesh are still part of us. Instead of following his statutes and living under his pavilion, we are constantly missing the link to connect to him for our eternity. We should pray and pray hard, never to miss joining Jesus in paradise. The fact is, no one in all these sins, like sexual immorality, impurity, sorcery, enmity, anger, unforgiveness, drunkenness, and hypocrisy. To kill others from our thoughts for the flesh, we cannot enter the kingdom of God.

On the contrary, as he has been repeating many things many times for our benefits, living for God through his Spirit that lives in you and me as the Holy Spirit gives us his fruit to live in his presence with love, joy, peace, patience, kindness, goodness, and faithfulness, leading us all into righteousness to heaven. If we live solely and totally depend on him for all our needs, he will supply them to our satisfaction, which will surpass our understanding due to the weight of his love toward us.

Loving him and loving the people caution us how to separate the children as the immigration rule around May to June 2018, when about two thousand children were separated from their parents. The rule is against innocent children as a punishment not resonating with American people and against the current president that Evangelicals need to speak out to help these children and their parents to benefit them both before God.

Depending on our accomplishments and thoughts to live for the devil, he had shown us so many punishments, which we call natural or Mother Nature's disasters. Now we are going to go through some rules many will not understand, and it has started already; we should be careful of war also prompted from him. Now our payback is here, and we can't do anything about it. Only repentance, prayers and fasting will move God to come to our aid. Yet time is not on our side. Jesus, can come, and God is showing so many signs and wonders to move us to a safer side by refraining from all unrighteousness when living for God.

Beloved people of God, if we make amends to our God, the safer that would be for us. Let's make the right choices to stay connected with our heavenly Father. He had repeatedly and candidly reminded us everything concerning sin, commandments, and repentance, especially the American people. Know that when persuasion fails, force of punishment must surely prevail. God helps us in our weaknesses. Oh, our first love, in you we dwell and have our being with your grace, which is sufficient for us, joining our faith to move every obstacle we face.

On June 7, 2015, on my prayer time as usual at around 10:30 p.m. to 12:30 p.m., I fell asleep only to be woken up at 1:00 a.m. to hear laughter about things that I should write down. And this happened oftentimes that he asked, "My daughter, have you heard that man's needs can be chosen over mine, my will, and my needs concerning what the leaders have done?" This is very incredible to him, how we are too stubborn as his image and how he is not stubborn. Without our enemy, this stubbornness will die naturally, and it will be our Father God and us.

None of us is supposed to have an idol. Put God first in our lives. Your idol is someone you love more than God, such as your wife, husband, son, daughter, father, or mother.

He was the first to love us all, and we should return his love before anyone else in our lives. This is it; our transitional period of being on earth is coming to an end. God will open the Book of Life and give his judgment, and Jesus will be on the throne to rule us. All that we have been going through will be no more, and our adversary, the devil, will be locked away forever.

Now joining Jesus will be those who will pass the judgment through all that were in the Bible. No more vices, no more sins to attract forgiveness, no more tears and pains. And no more trials and tribulations and proving for any crown. They will all be things of the past.

In this new world, all the good and obedient lifestyles we practiced will matter, such as accepting Jesus as the Son of God, who died and rose again to bring us salvation by grace, he who has given us the humility to enter his rest and to enjoy all that the Father has for our entry into the new world.

While those who did their own thing without regard for God's commandments and plans will be locked in the pit of fire with their master of the former world, now will be the turn of true Christians to enjoy the tranquility and serene atmosphere in paradise, just like in the garden that we lost. I am sure paradise is greater than the garden with many things.

We love Jesus and love the Father, and we become the children who have been born of God. Having been born of God makes us the overcomers of the world, which transforms us to live in the first world that was full of temptation. But due to the true love of God, we lived under his commandments, kept His ordinances, and was mindful of his precepts that had earned us the new second world. We will be ruling with Jesus to reap our joy we lost in the first world by forgetting the flesh and living for the Spirit of the living God—who was, is, and is to come again to join us in this new world. Remember, He gave us eternal life in the Son forever.

Imagine that those of us who passed the judgment are in the new world, full of peace. We are going to walk in the truth by living according to the truth we saw in the Bible—loving God with all our hearts, minds, and emotions without any interruption whatsoever, like how it was in the former world. Then living with that faithfulness and righteousness gives joy to the same people. All struggles will be forever gone. We can now start dreaming about the second world and be anxious to live right with anticipation to do all that it takes to join Jesus.

We are going to prosper with purpose without any hindrance in our spiritual growth as before. There will be spiritual maturity that he created for us to grow fully in mind, will, and emotions and to think with the mind of Jesus Christ through the Word of God. And there will be no more tricks into confusion—ideas and thoughts of a woman wanting to be a man or a man wanting to be a woman as if we humans invented the creation and as if God were under our instructions to make mistakes and that we even debate about colors and race. And no more ideas of putting the most expensive spermatozoa into the most waste products of the body to kill babies and dirty our image and produce diseases.

There will be no more of such things to come to mind and pump us up for consideration; nothing of that sort will exist again, never. There will only be healthy relationships between a man and a woman, which God has designed for us, since Satan, our adversary, would not be there to poke and confuse us with thoughts.

The nation that trusts in the Lord comes on board with things like what our predecessors left for us. We may live like those who wholeheartedly lived for God and were called to eternal life, such as the American pastor and evangelist Billy Graham, who passed away in February 2018.

Our Father will welcome him home, saying, "Well done, good and faithful servant," without any grief but only happiness and enjoyment. Start dreaming of the second world, and start changing from being sinful and greedy to having righteous living for God and putting God first in all things we do, is what he requires from us.

Other than that, a great nation like America became miserable when our president betrayed us before the world, where he believed in the Russian president more than his own intelligence like the CIA on the result of the investigation of the 2016 elections' cyber meddling. Today, July 16, 2018, has been our miserable day when I heard some saying treason while watching CNN. Does this confirms his slogan of America First? That is all what God is trying to call our attention about, that if the branch leaves the vine, it becomes weak. And unhappy things are happening to us in our great nation now. Let's include God very seriously to continue to enjoy our glory before the world like before. Let's learn a lesson from this.

The ultimate God Almighty directed me to write this book, knowing my heart toward Him how when I see how majority of mankind instead of bringing him the glory He deserves bring him pains and grieves, which let me also drop many tears. I am a human being too and am subject to fall into sin, especially when I was young. But for a long time now, I am very cautious to be guided by the good book, the Bible, to do what it is teaching us.

I pray that mankind would also be cautious and follow all that the Bible is telling us to know and live for the One who created us mindful of why we are here and where we go from here. We are bound by the dos and don'ts on our existence here to glorify God for whom all things are created for his glory, concerning our lives of test and trust, which will be the way we handle our assignments and how to pass to the next level.

Our knowledge of the temporary citizenship on this planet Earth disallows us to fight tooth and nail for all the wealth of the world greedily, and to commit us into many sins. The aim or awareness of the con man Satan and the role he plays with his cohorts is to incriminate us to lose our connection with our Master and Creator, turning our relationship of peace into war of sins and robbing us of the unconditional love bestowed by the never-giving-up God.

What to do by prayers and meditation on the Word plus righteousness and right standing with God through salvation to be where we belong, as permanent citizens of heaven.

> Dear heavenly Father, thank you for creating and allowing us to live on this planet Earth with all the beautiful things for us to manage and keep for accountability. Thank you for knowing how sinful we are, yet you never gave up on us and mindful of working on us to perfection, enabling us to fulfill our purposes

that you put into every one of us. For none of us was mistakenly created but uniquely, wonderfully made as your masterpiece.

O gracious Father, we thank you for remembering us in our low state, giving food to all flesh and quickening the stronger and richer ones to take care of the poor and vulnerable ones. Thank you for your loving kindness, mercy, and grace that is sufficient for us. You fought our battles for us to hold our peace, gave vengeance and justice to the wicked for the righteous, and delivered us out of all our troubles as we see us triumph over all our enemies.

Help us in our weaknesses and deliver us from all the evil intentions of our enemies. And may we live for your glory to be shown on earth. As we fulfill our purpose, I pray that you listen to our prayers and send us to heaven to deliver us from all the battles of our enemies as you sent your only Son to die and rise for our redemption, performing on our behalf, protecting, delivering, and healing us from all the diseases the enemy have inflicted on those who know their God. And with your help, we do exploits. Glory, honor, and adoration belong to you. There is none like You, who created and delivered us from death. Help our feet from falling into temptations that we will walk before you, O Lord, as all the earth bow down and sing praises to your name, seeing the wonderful works of your hands. Since You have an expected end for us and not evil, Jeremiah 29:11-12.

Be exalted, God the Father, the Son, and the Holy Spirit, forming the Trinity. Be exalted above the heavens and let your glory be shown over all the earth forever. I pray in Jesus's mighty name. Amen.

If in any case our right is superior to that of our Father God's right, then it's wrong. Who will take care of our physical and spiritual needs? Ponder over this well. A group of people or an individual should properly evaluate the following and be convinced with the answers before concluding they are doing the right things. And if not, then they might be entitled to their opinion, being the enemy using their mind as the battlefield for his agenda that leads to their doom. Helpful evaluation for guidance to know our position here will help in our decision-making and convince us to our better lifestyles based on logic.

1. Do you know who created all the things you are seeing and enjoying, like the earth, the air we breathe, the water we drink, the oceans with fish, the rain, the forests and animals, the snow, and the weather throughout the year—the entire creation and the mysteries behind them?

2. Have you taken time to evaluate the entire concept of how your father's sperm swam to catch one egg in your mother's womb for your birth as all mysterious?

3. The growth and development of your five senses where you see, touch, hear, taste, and smell till you grew to take that decision? As well as your height and knowing the number of your hair on your head, the development of your brain, the cerebrum, and the cerebellum as all part of the puzzle of the mysterious? All human developments start like a graph from our physical body and our intellects to age fifty to sixty and start to decline from almost all our formation, especially our brain, which loses some hormones and deteriorates fast with forgetfulness to our amazement.

4. The creation described the marriage between a man and a woman, and you came out of that. So how was that practice going to increase the world population to reach about 7.5 billion today?

If you can't answer yes to any of these questions, then you have failed and have no justification on your agenda to make this world a better place apart from the devil using your mind to be wicked to your partner to use him or her like a dog to breed sickness, caring less whether one dies or lives. And it is not love that had joined you together but selfishness, thinking about your own interest, which is taking you to hell (Proverbs 14:29–35). Now that you know, pray every day with your partner to God to deliver you both from the grip of the devil to change your lifestyles and go to a Bible-believing church for your salvation. Or say, "Lord Jesus, I repent of my sins. Come into my heart. Cleanse me from all unrighteousness, and I will make you my Lord and Savior."

Then start immediately to read your Bible—three chapters first thing in the morning and last thing to go to bed, plus one psalm a day from the book of Psalms, meditating on those and touching your hearts to know the truth to drive the devil away from you and be free. Then start fasting at least for the first seven days for purification to drive the devil away fast. Fasting could be from 6:00 a.m. to 10:00 a.m., 6:00 a.m. to 12:00 noon or to 3:00 p.m., depending on your strength. Be sure to drink water or do Daniel's kind of fasting, eating only salads and vegetables (Daniel 10:3). Beloved, let the truth set you free than be a slave to sin. Apply the blood of Jesus to cancel and disconnect the devil's tricks to lure you back and forth into his domain for future suffering with him.

Hold your hands and pray that God should bring you the woman he took from your flesh, bone, and blood. He will do it now that you have accepted Jesus as your Lord and Savior. The Holy Spirit has come to live in you and will be prompting you from committing anything unhealthy. So be attentive to the gentle, still voice. Join a Bible-believing church near you, and see the pastor for counseling and for the Holy Spirit's baptism to speak in tongues. This way, you can pray to yourselves all the time. The devil is afraid of that and will sooner run away. Remember, you were born into the world's family of mankind. And now through Jesus, you have been connected to the family of God to belong to a Bible-believing Church of Jesus Christ and to believe what the Bible is teaching us.

May God help you on your new transitions to the light of His healthy relationship in Jesus's mighty name. Amen. Without being strong with willpower, he will come back with mighty agents. Now you have been born of God and have overcome the world of malice. Keep on staying strong in righteousness as you guide and help other friends to go into the same transition. Congratulations to those with a change of heart and are prepared to go to heaven and meet the Father in paradise, the chance to the second world. The New Jerusalem is guaranteed where Jesus himself will govern.

No more evil temptations, no more death and fear of abominable practices. The light will always conquer darkness. For the master of the darkness, being in the spiritual world, had captured the souls of the people he forced into sin and are already in his prison till they die to face judgment, making them comfortable with sin until you go to a Bible-believing church for deliverance with a strong willpower or determination as God will reach out to you in victory.

In the second world (afterlife), we will be at liberty to enjoy all the promises. Since all things come from God alone, all things live for his glory as he made all things for his own purpose. His goal of the universe is to showcase His nature, the magnitude of his importance, the radiance of his splendor, the demonstration of his power, and the atmosphere of his presence to know that all glory belongs to him. God's glory, which he doesn't share with any of his creations, is the expression of Him and all his goodness. Other intrinsic and all the qualities of all things created by Him when we look around, reflect who he is as he planned to create us like himself for his pleasure to enjoy before we were lost in the garden.

You are now a new creation as you surrender totally to Jesus Christ. You will be fed on a silver spoon to start with. Start reading your Bible in a year to allow Genesis to help you in your choices; Exodus to learn how God will bring you out of your troubles, meaning deliverance; and Leviticus to learn how to obey God for your blessings. They go on and on till you reach Revelation to acquaint yourself with the world coming to an end, being caught in the rapture. Then evaluate your choice to make a cross of happiness to be among the saints.

Having this knowledge, reach out to all your friends and loved ones at any cost and help them to see the light revealed to souls for their blessings. Just like when you were practicing, you were enticing others to be like you. Male to male or female to female. Now advocating for the truth, it has been revealed to you like how God created Adam and took his rib and brought Eve. Therefore, he said a man will leave his parents and join the woman and be one flesh.

Your past failed relationship does not give you license to connect to the same gender, which is not love but hatred, sending you in the perpetual fire forever and ever, so escape.

The gospel's truth is how we can classify love as sex and do something to your neighbor that can endanger his life, thus contradicting what God originally created. Now you know the truth to set you free. Immediately, you feel remorse and return to him. He would love to forgive you all and will not remember your sins anymore. He keeps on telling you throughout the book how he is waiting for you to come back to him as soon as possible. Since he had not revealed the day of rapture to anyone, it will come like a thief in the night for the destruction of those who hardened their hearts and refused to listen like they own the world. It will be great for those who have ears to listen and those who have not refused.

Those who were not sick did not need Jesus for any healing. Knowing that you are sick of any kind of sin or real sickness, you become a friend of Jesus, developing a friendship with him to be more than any other friend. He is closer to you than any other friend and will do what no friend can do for you, which money often could not do. Love him with all your heart, mind, soul, and spirit and see that your path will be directed with great love, being sin-free and having inner peace and joy each day. Forget all you have done. He wants you in any situation just as you are to come to him. He is saying, "You are mine." Now pray for your wife or husband to come and build your family to honor and to be grateful for the love only he can give.

Toward the conclusion, I waited on the Lord God to round up the book for me, and he provided this through WhatsApp to my amazement. And I quote with the heading "European Court of Human Rights: Human Rights That Homosexual Marriage Is Not a Human Right," with a picture of a young guy who did it for money and got the money but died with anal cancer, looking like a shameful skeleton. Very pitiful.

> Unanimously, the Human Rights Court of Strasbourg, France—the world court of human rights—has established, verbatim, that "there is no right to homosexual marriage." The forty-seven judges of the forty-seven countries of the Council of Europe, which are members of the full Court of Strasbourg (the world's most important human rights court), issued a statement of great relevance that has been surprisingly silenced by information progressivism and its area of influence. In fact, unanimously, the forty-seven judges approved the ruling that "there is no right to homosexual marriage." The sentence was based on a myriad of philosophical and anthropological considerations based on natural order, common sense, scientific reports, and of course, positive law, within the latter, in particular.

> The judgment was based on Article 12 of the European Convention on Human Rights. This is equivalent to the articles of human rights treaties, as in the case

of seventeen of the pacts of San Jose and no. 23 of the International Covenant on Civil and Political Rights. In this historic but not disclosed resolution, the court decided that the concept of the family not only contemplates "the traditional concept of marriage, that is, the union of a man and a woman, but also that they should not be imposed on governments to the obligation to open marriage to persons of the same sex." As for the principle of nondiscrimination, the court also added that there is no discrimination since "states are free to reserve marriage only to heterosexual couples."

It is important and necessary to spread this kind of news, but governments and sympathizers of such will not want people to know. Help spread the news if you want! And I found it on WhatsApp. Obviously, it does not interest the media to publicize the news. Coming to the end of this book that he told me to write, this showed that God has won this case: "God Almighty versus the People." This is amazing in Jesus's mighty name. Amen. He is the answer to every problem. Whoever reads this book and is baffled about anything should pray to God to give him the answer, him being the owner of this book who wants all his people to hear from him. He is our Creator; in him we live and have our being. We depend and trust him.